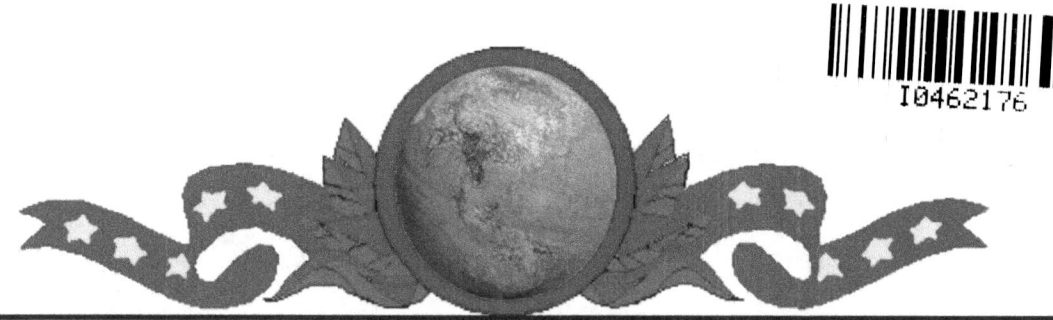

Real World
Colouring Book
For Advanced Users & Adults

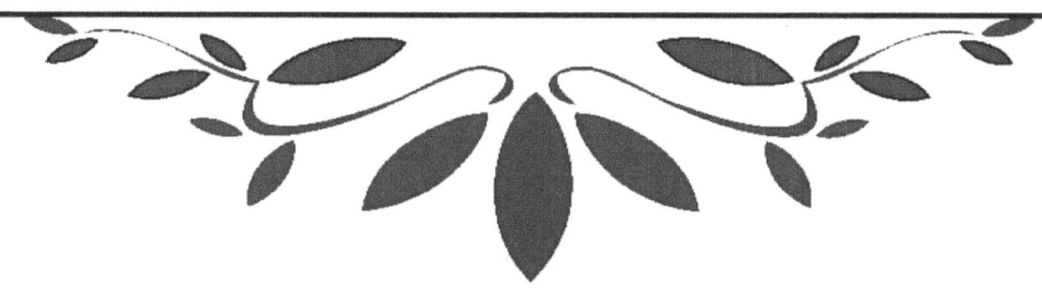

Copyright 2019 By John Boom

50 Images

Created From Real Life Photos
For You To Colour As You Please.

ISBN 978-0-359-82321-5
90000

9 780359 823215

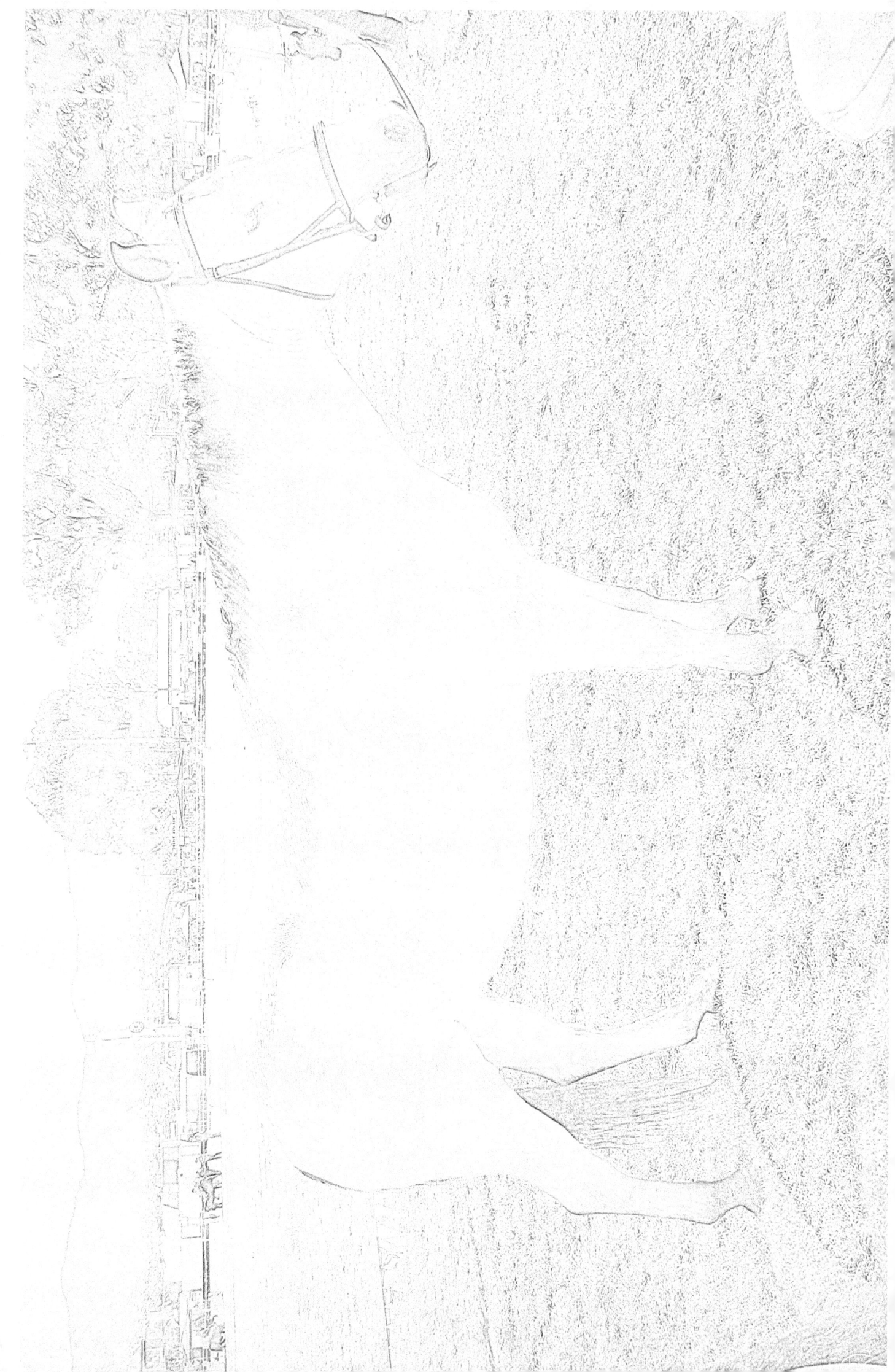

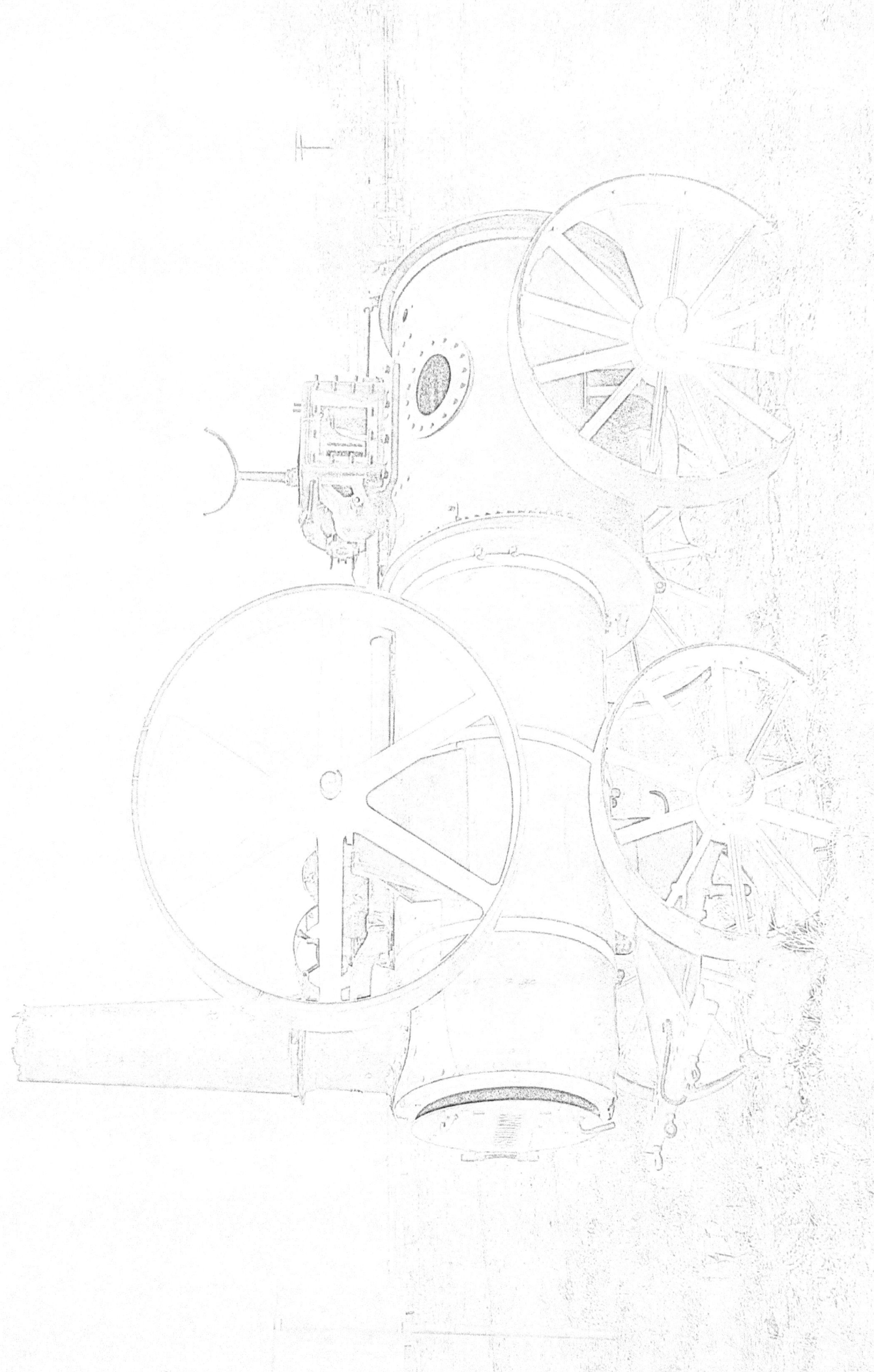

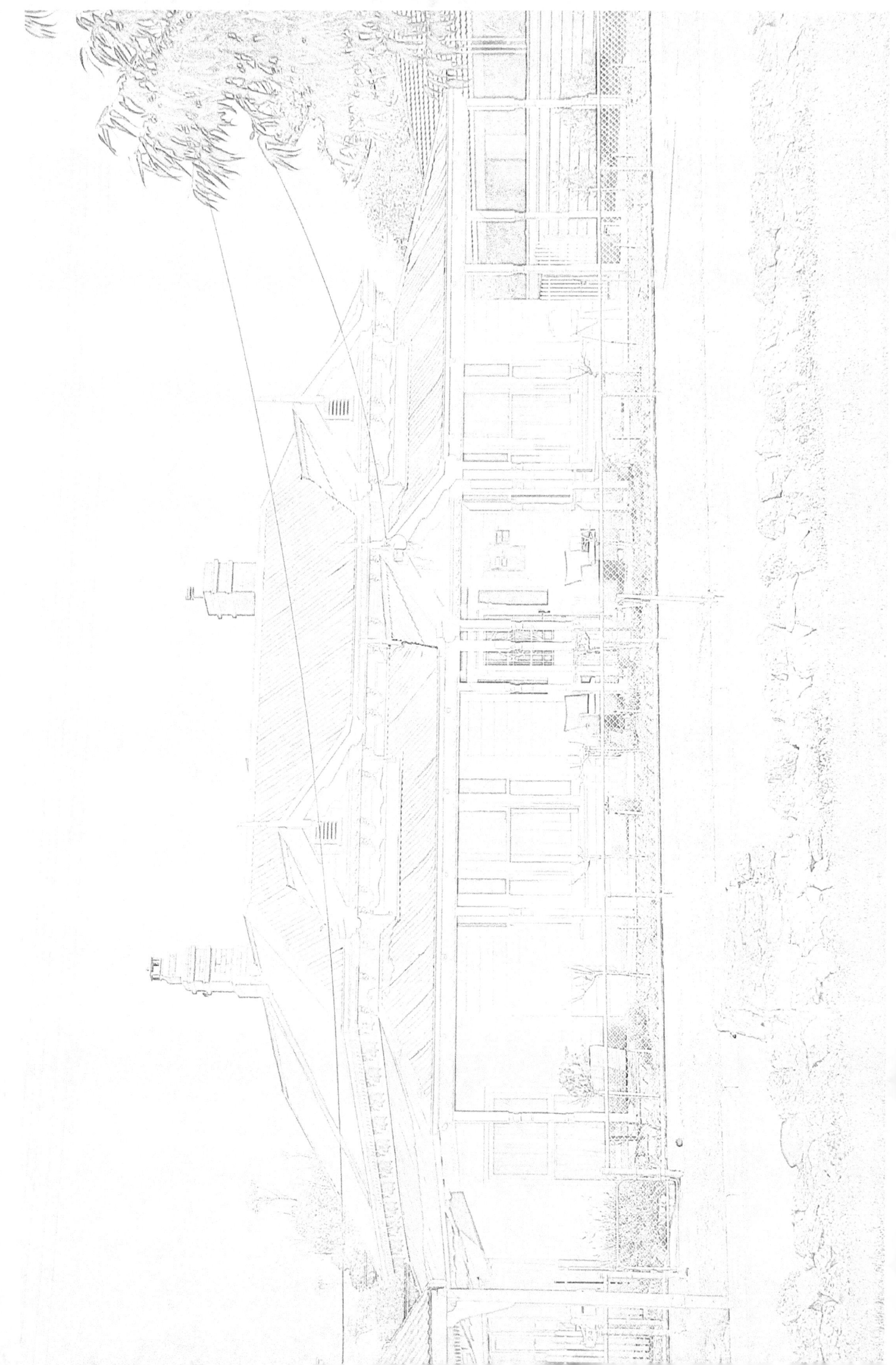

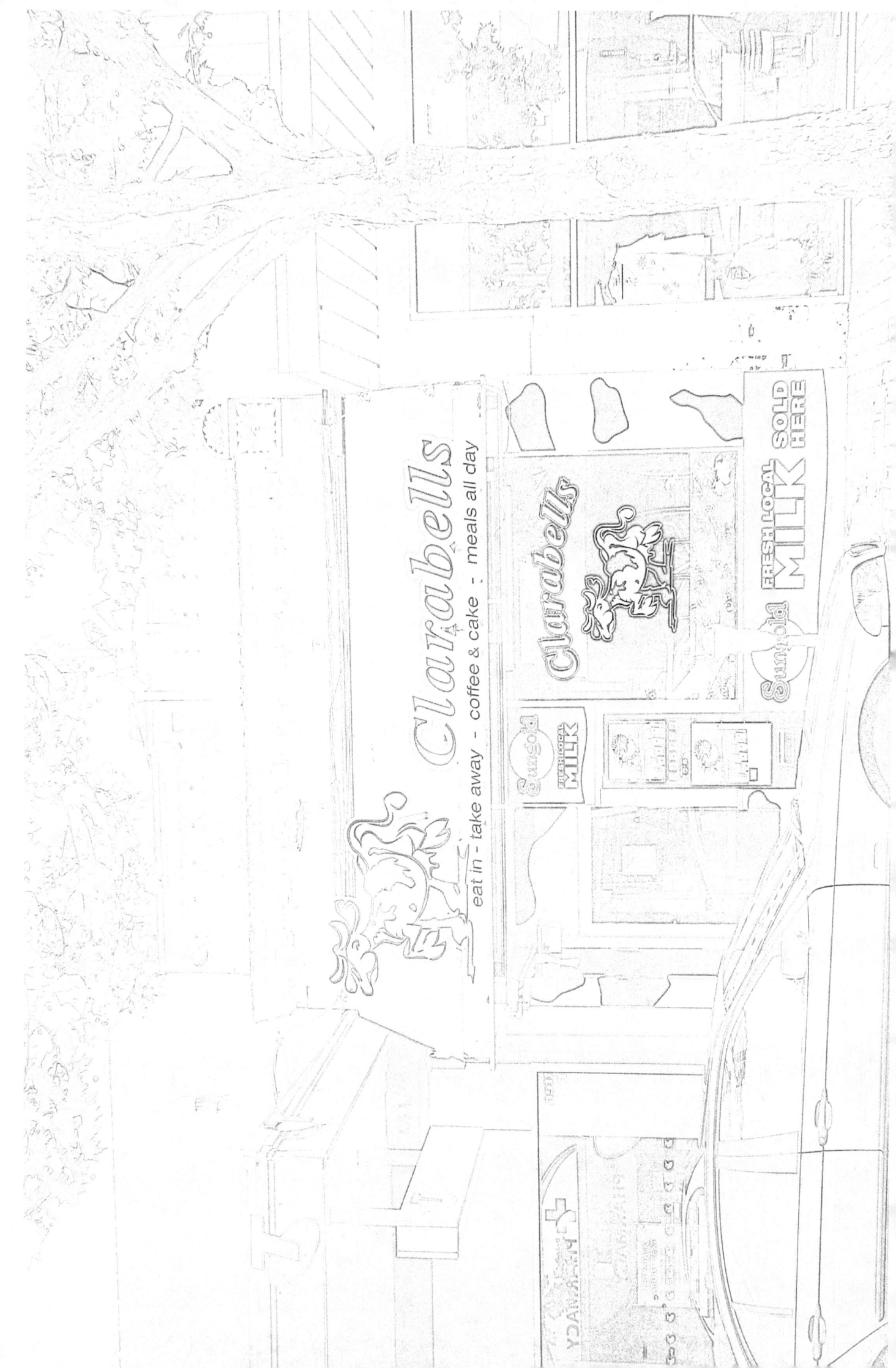

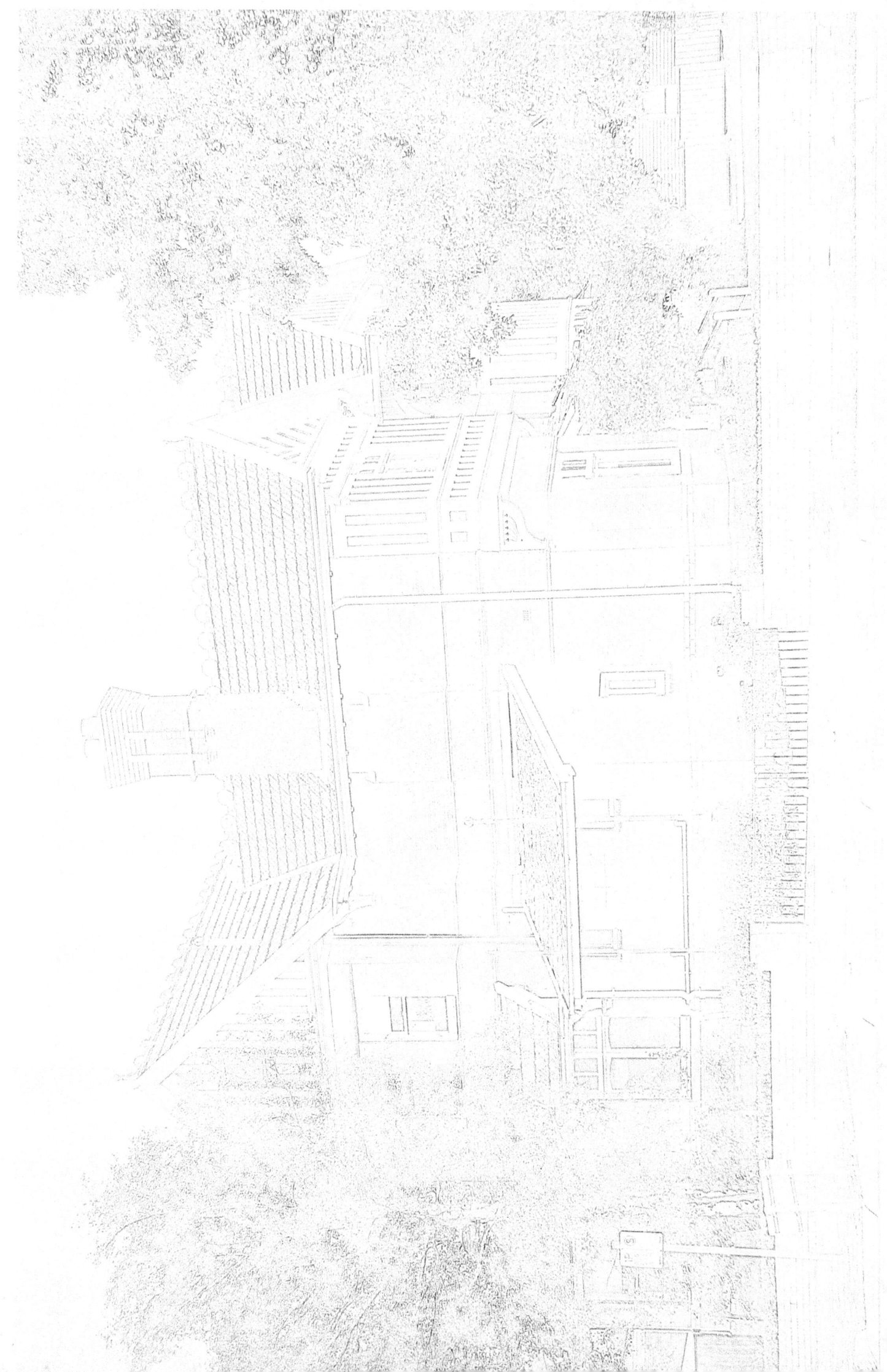

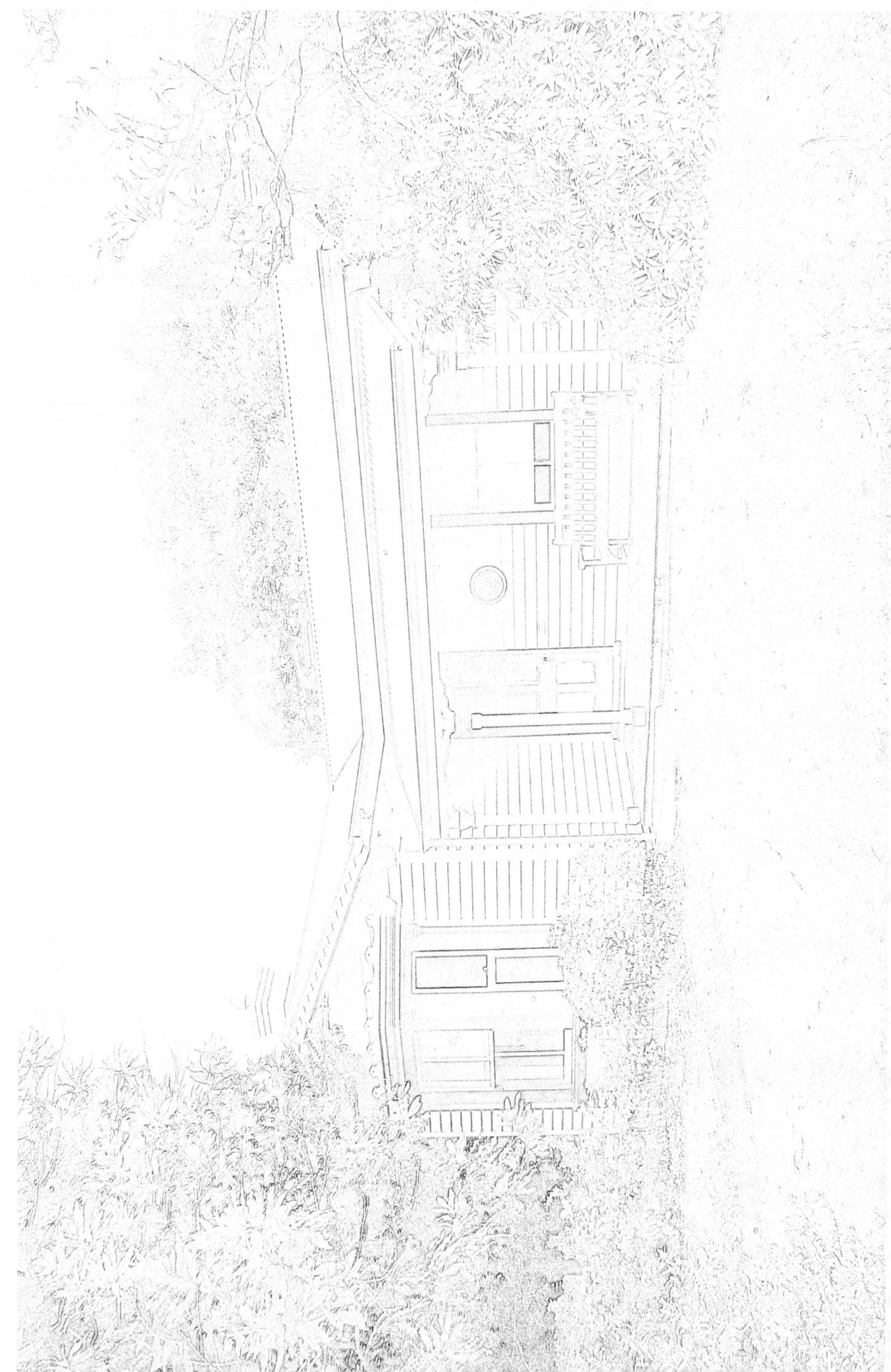

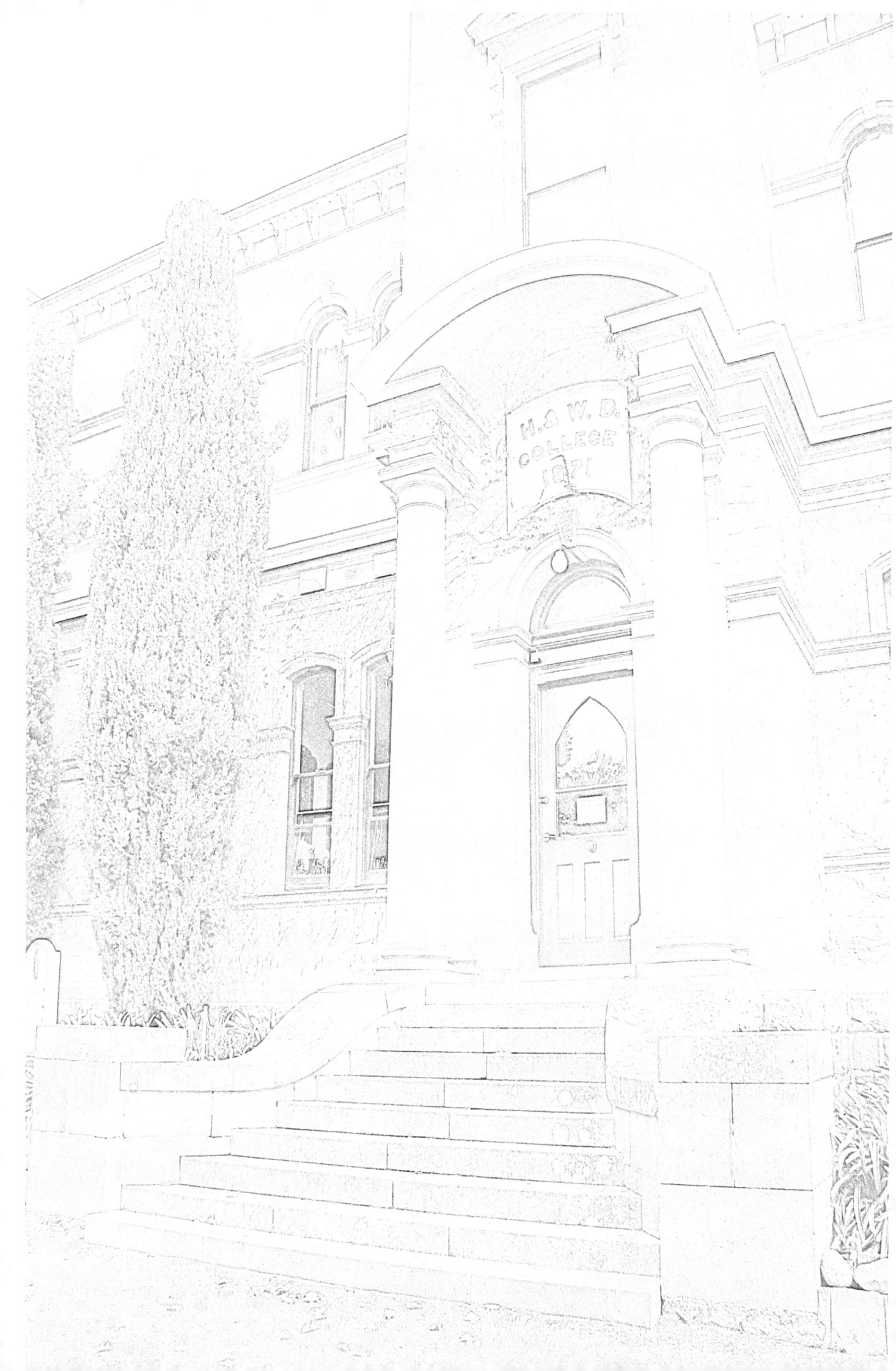

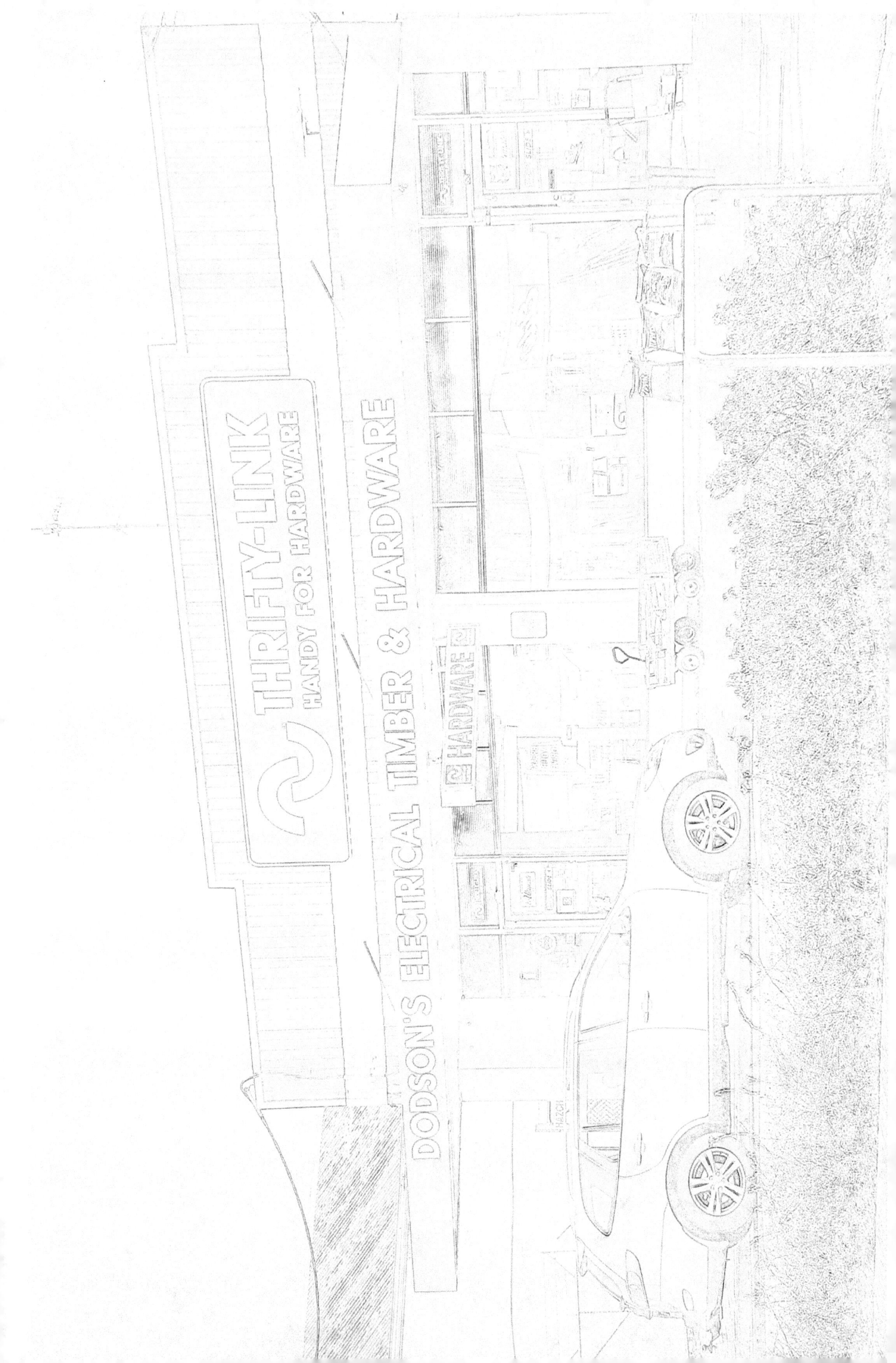

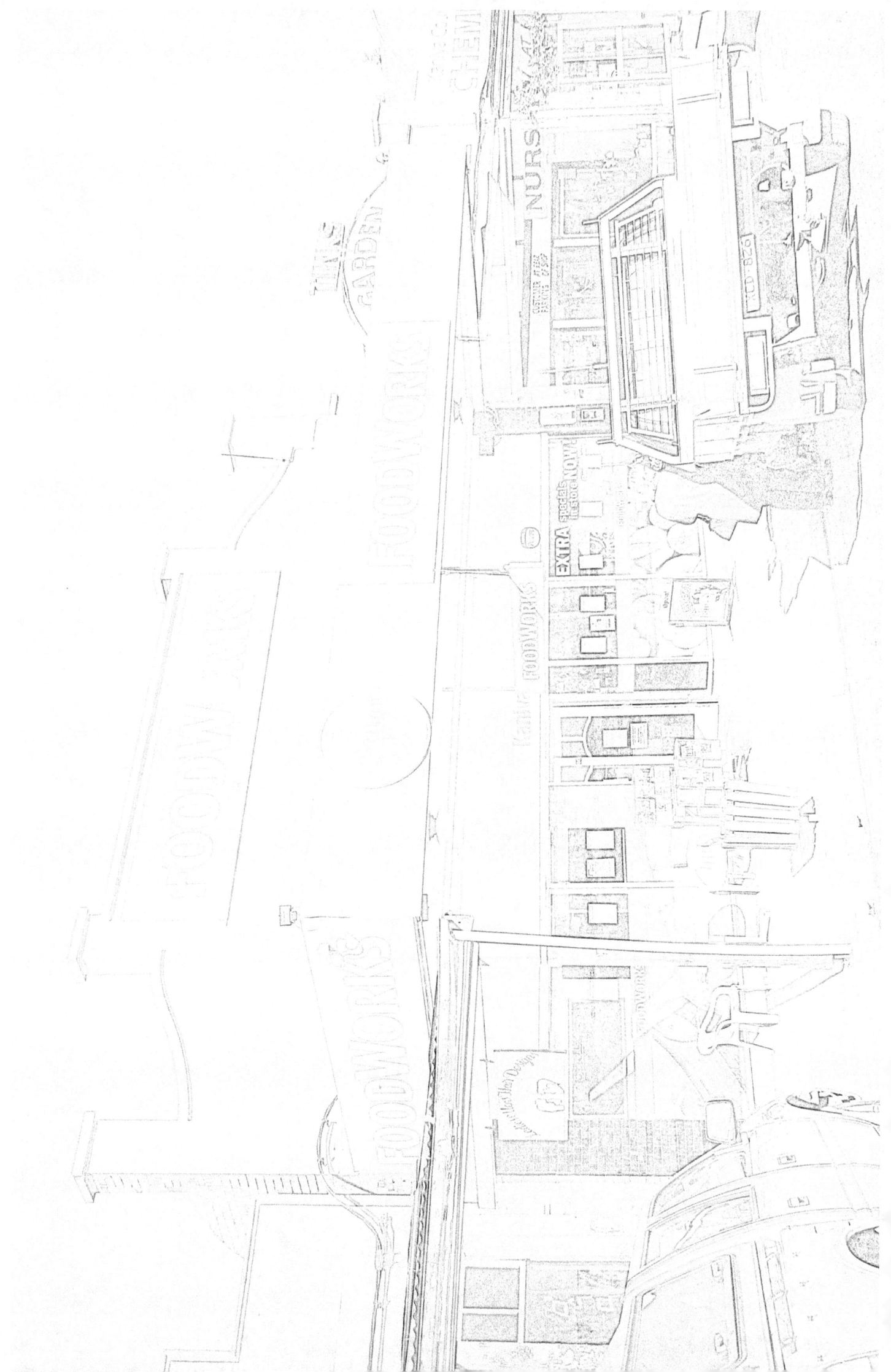

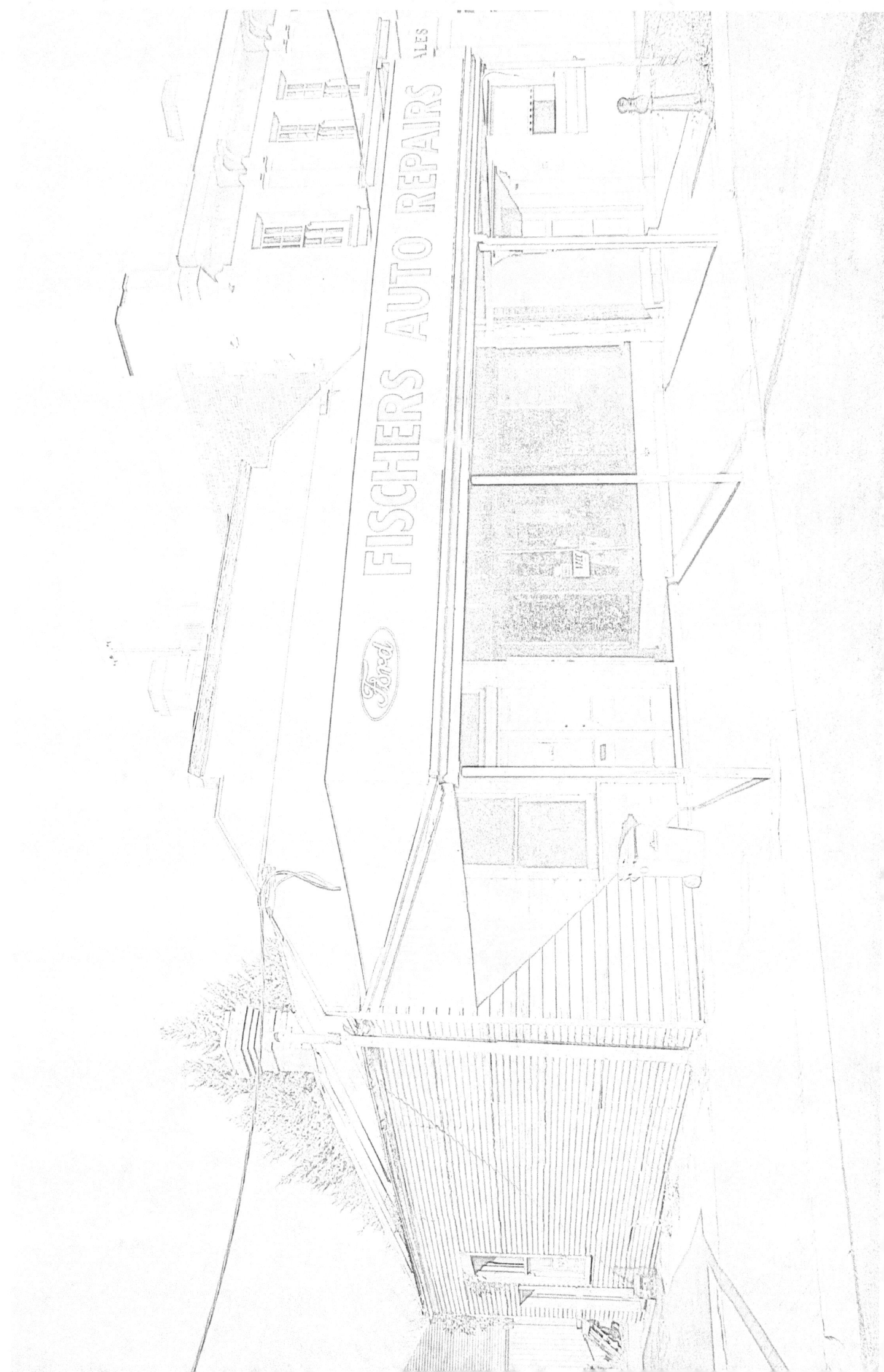

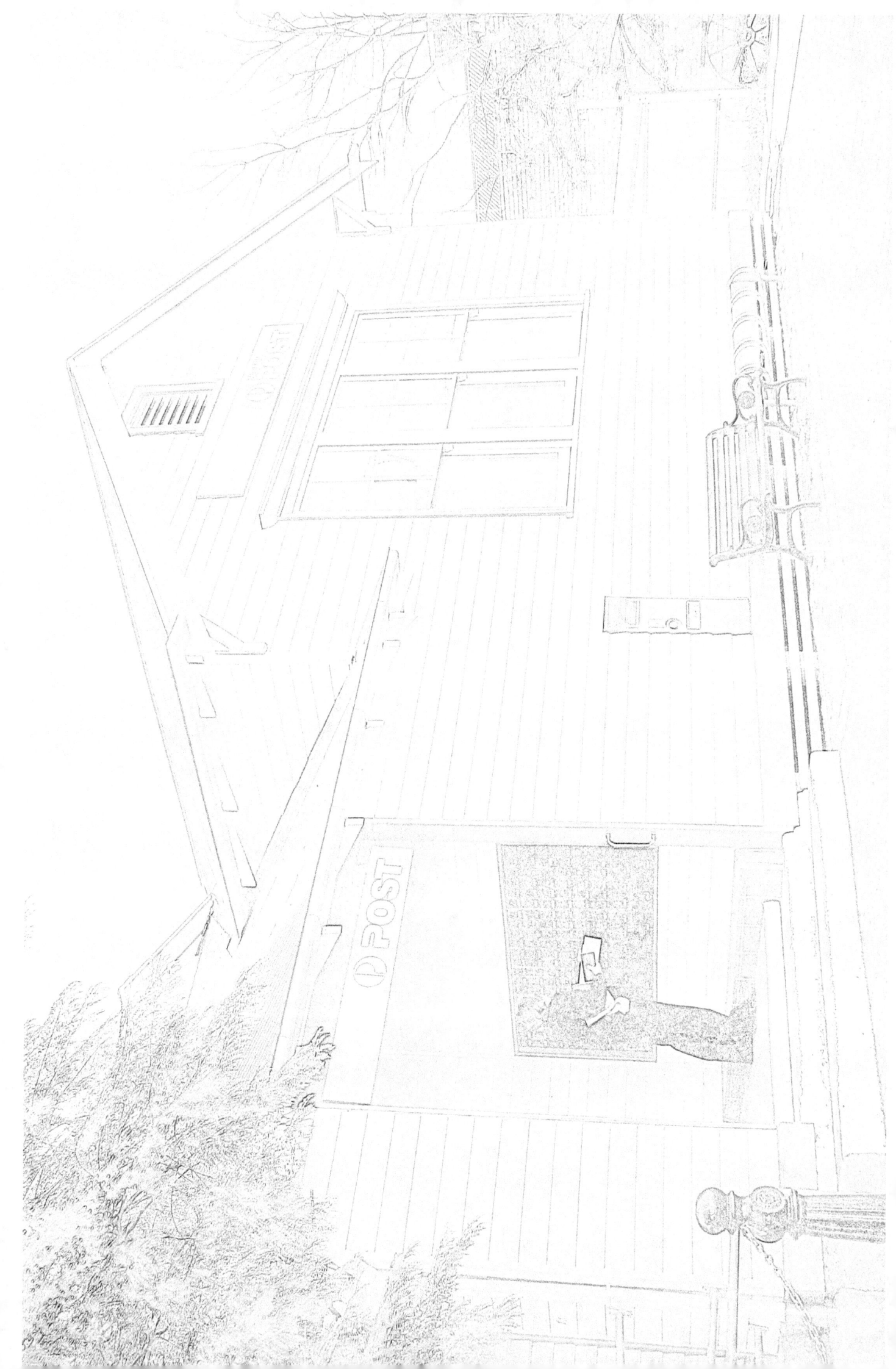

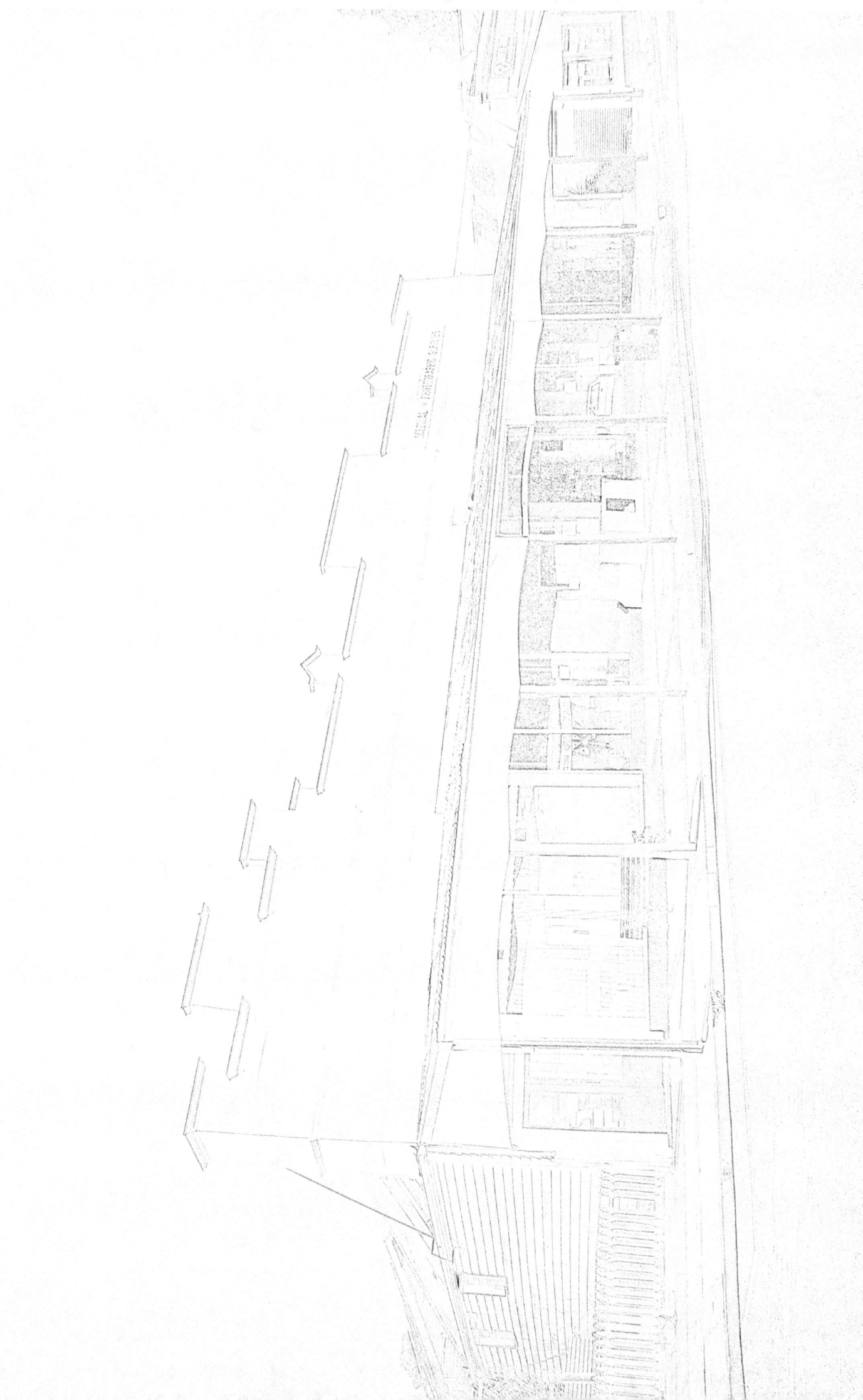

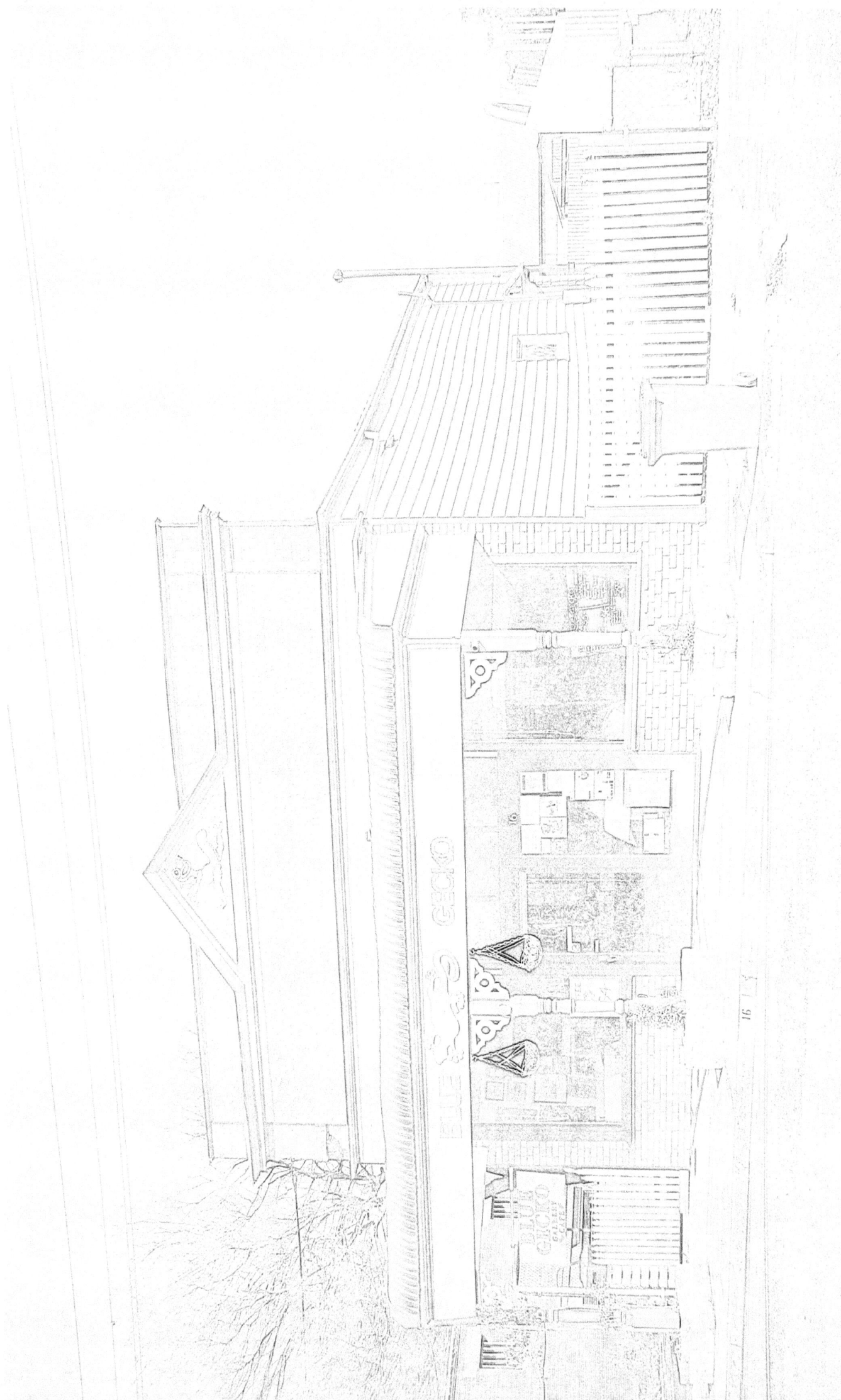

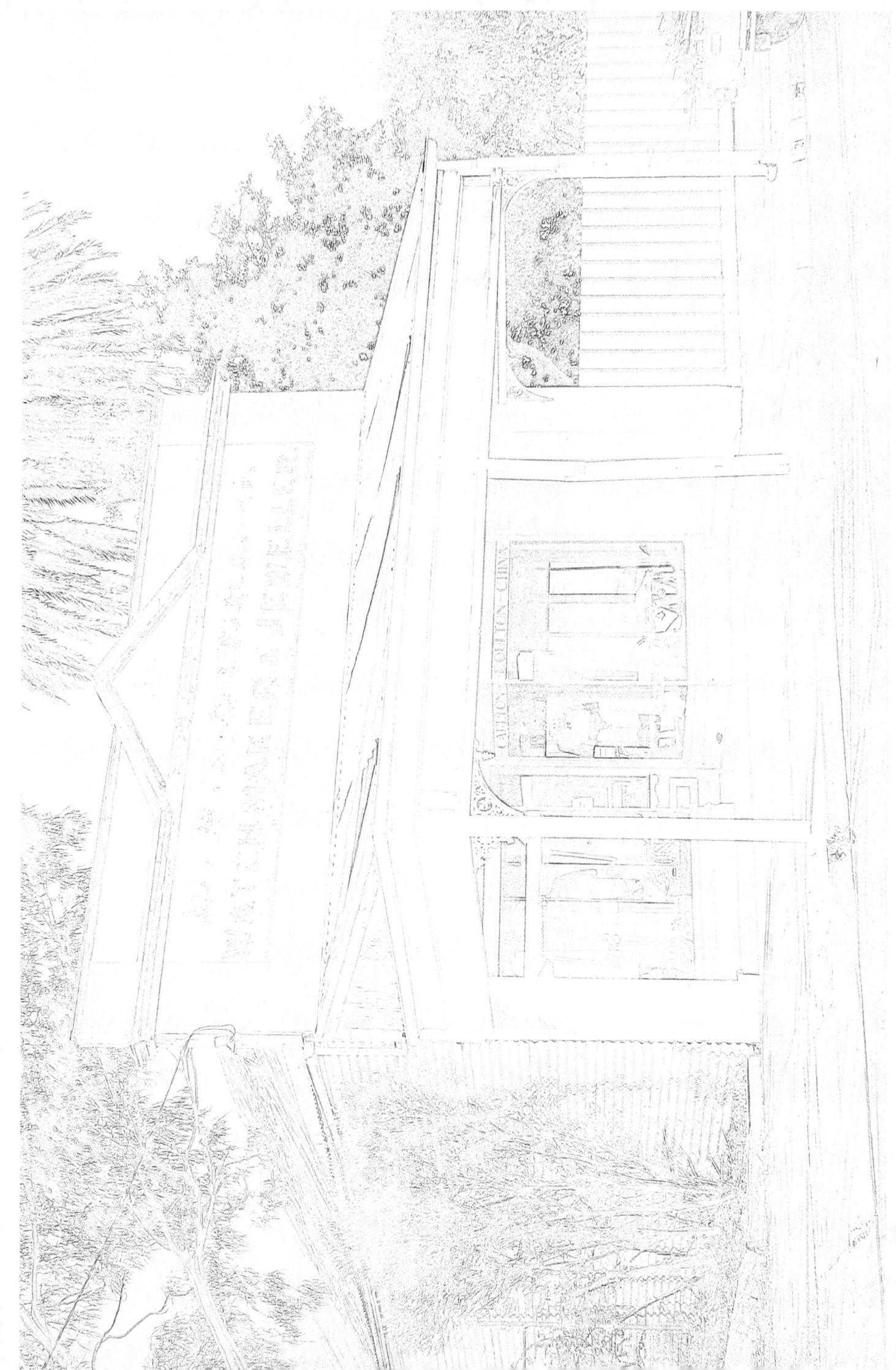

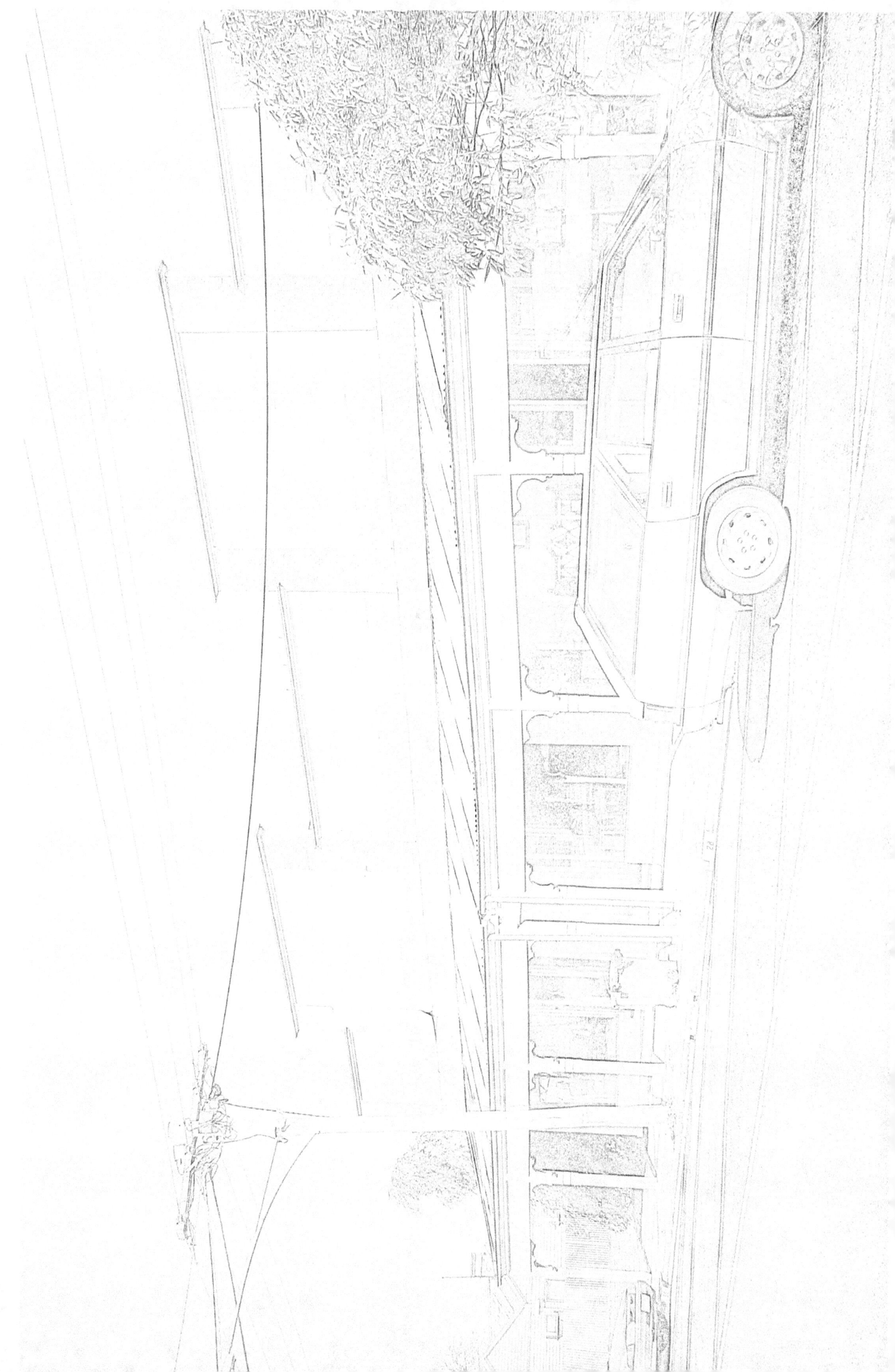

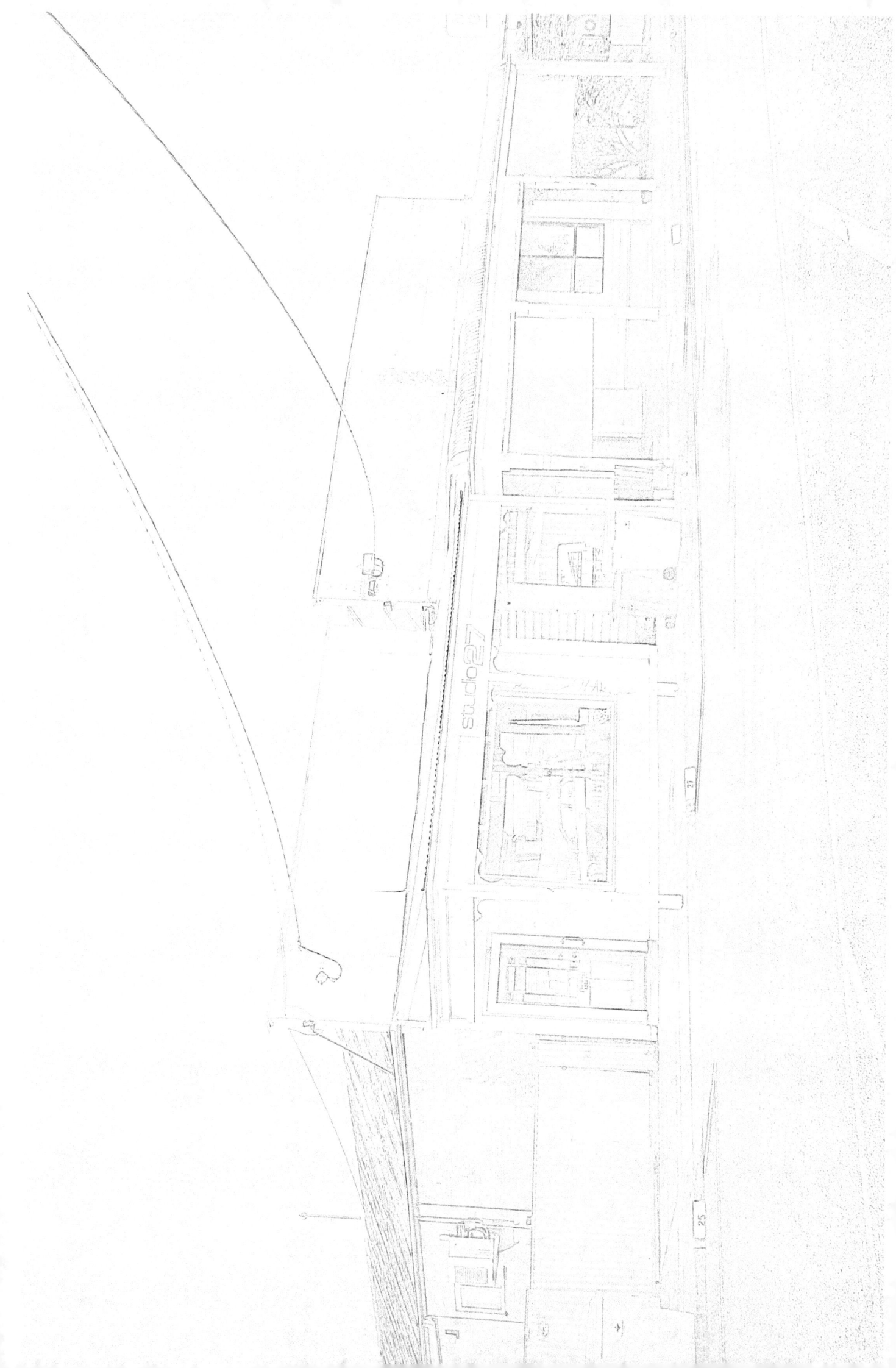

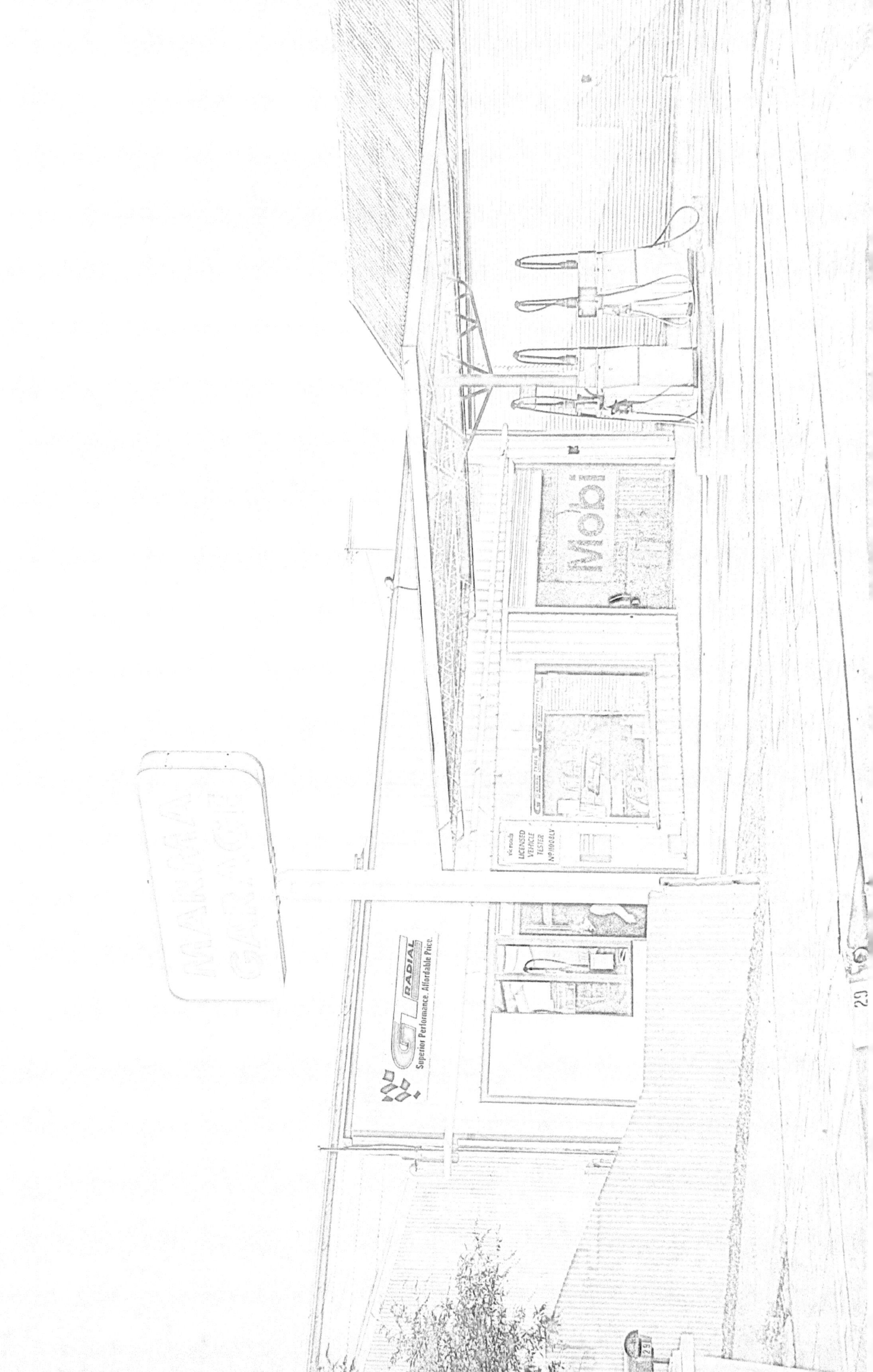

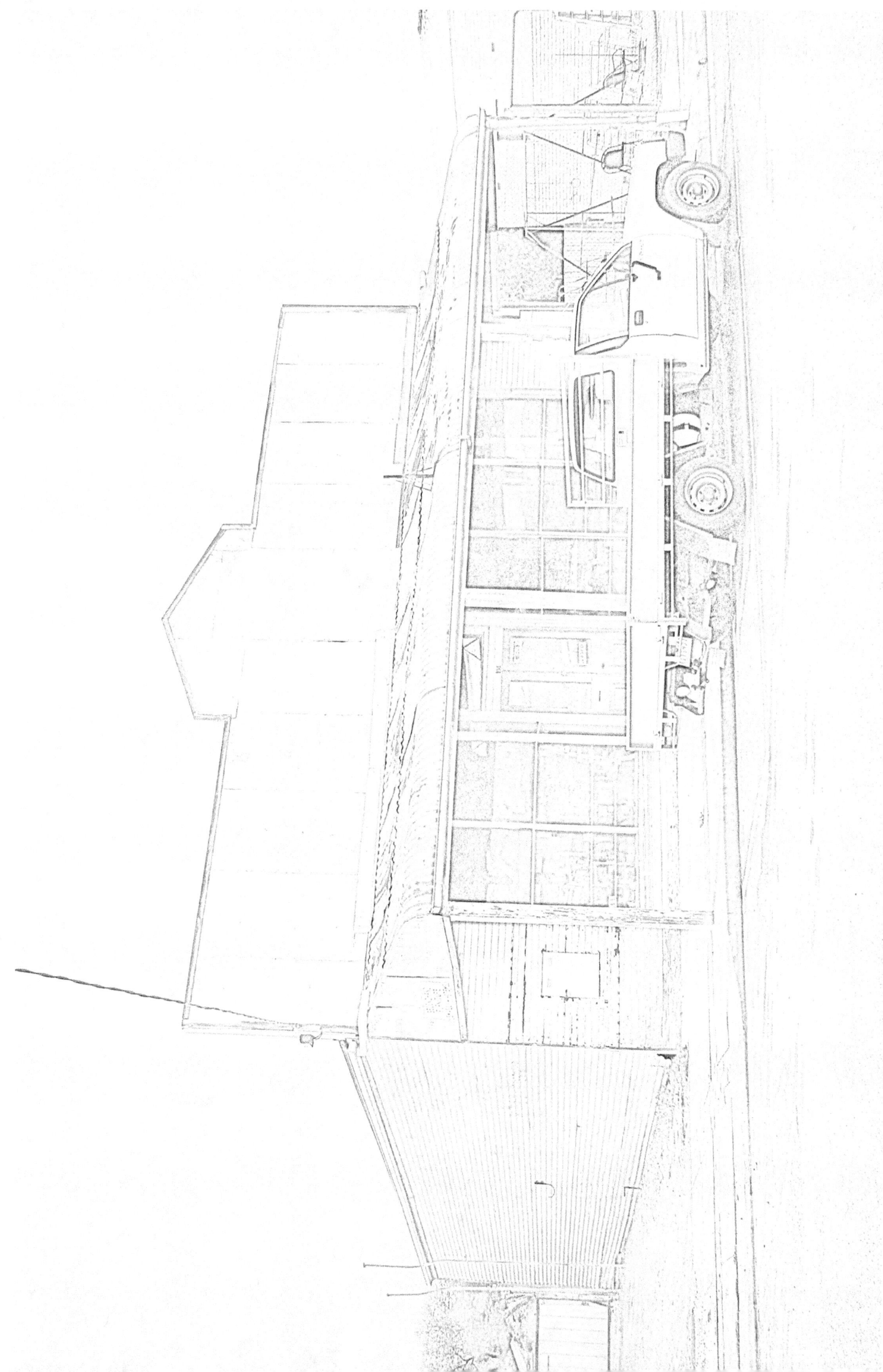

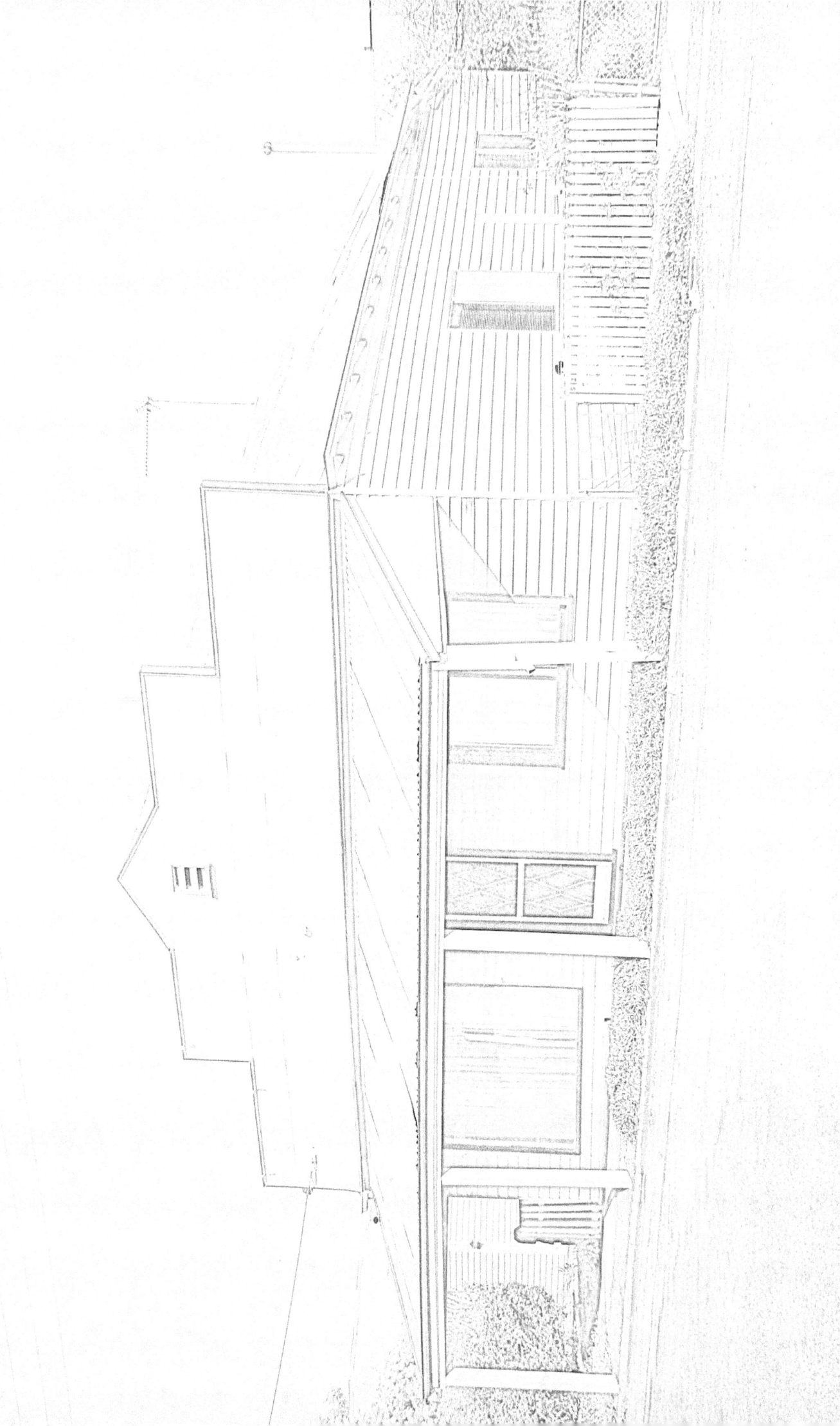

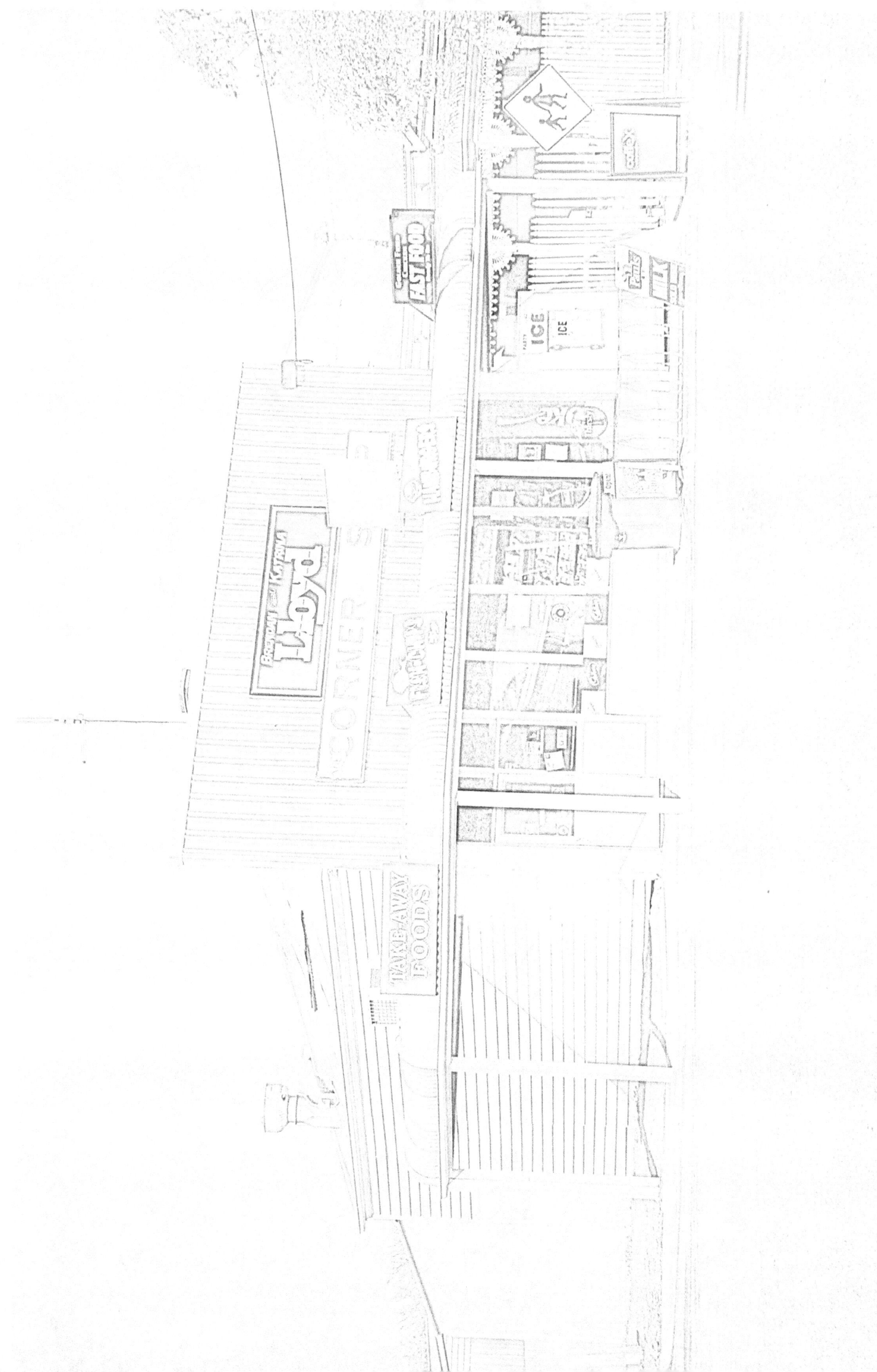

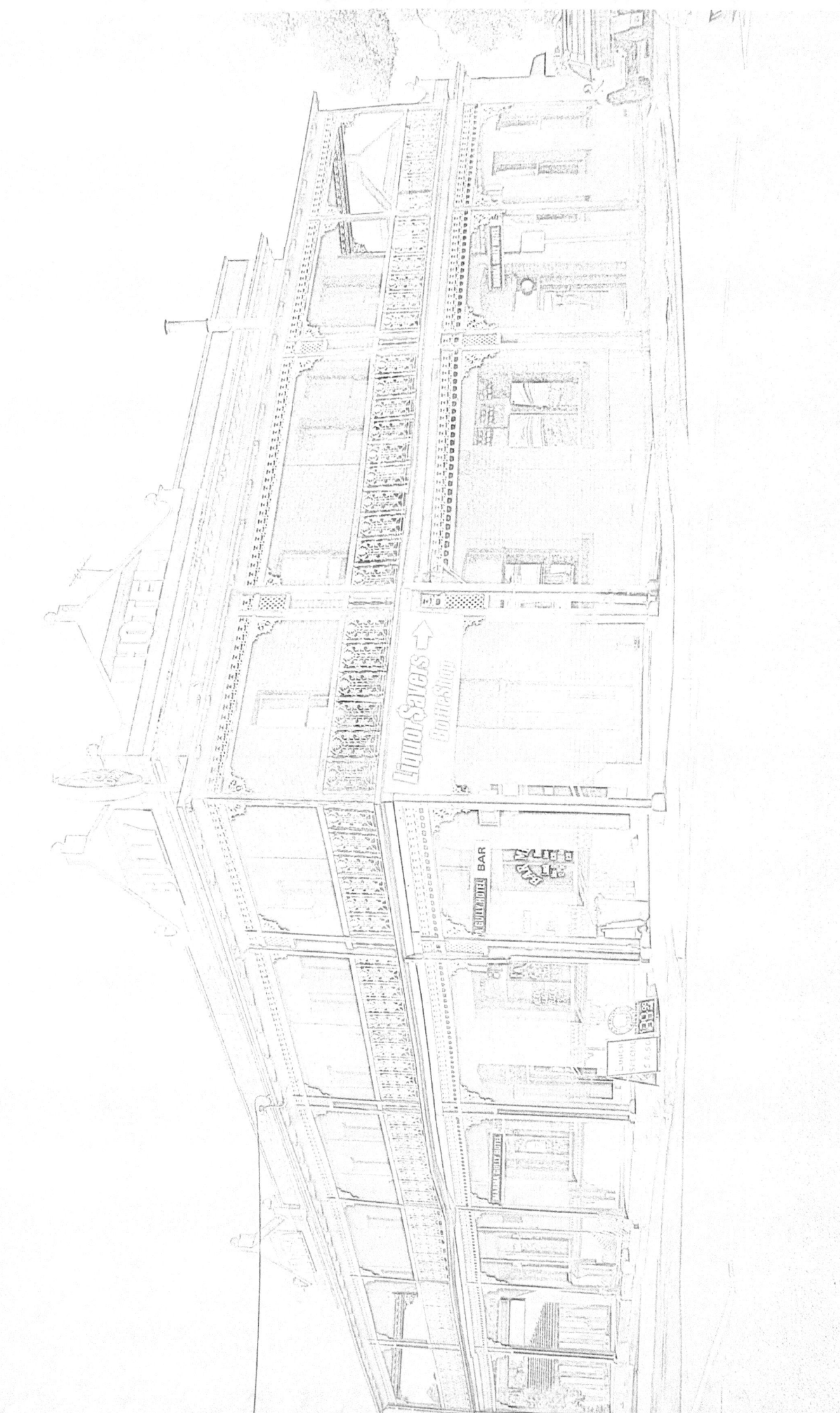

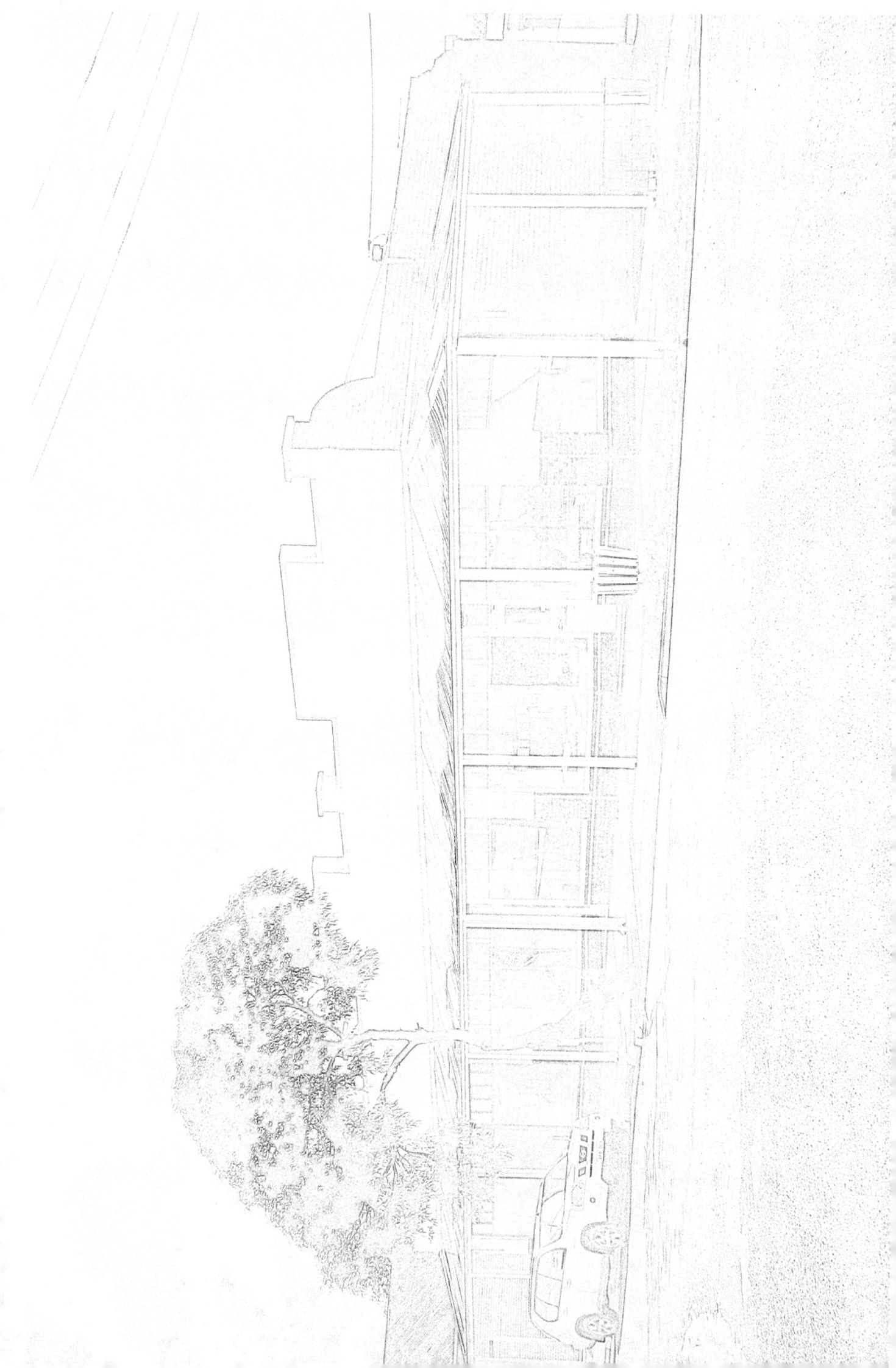

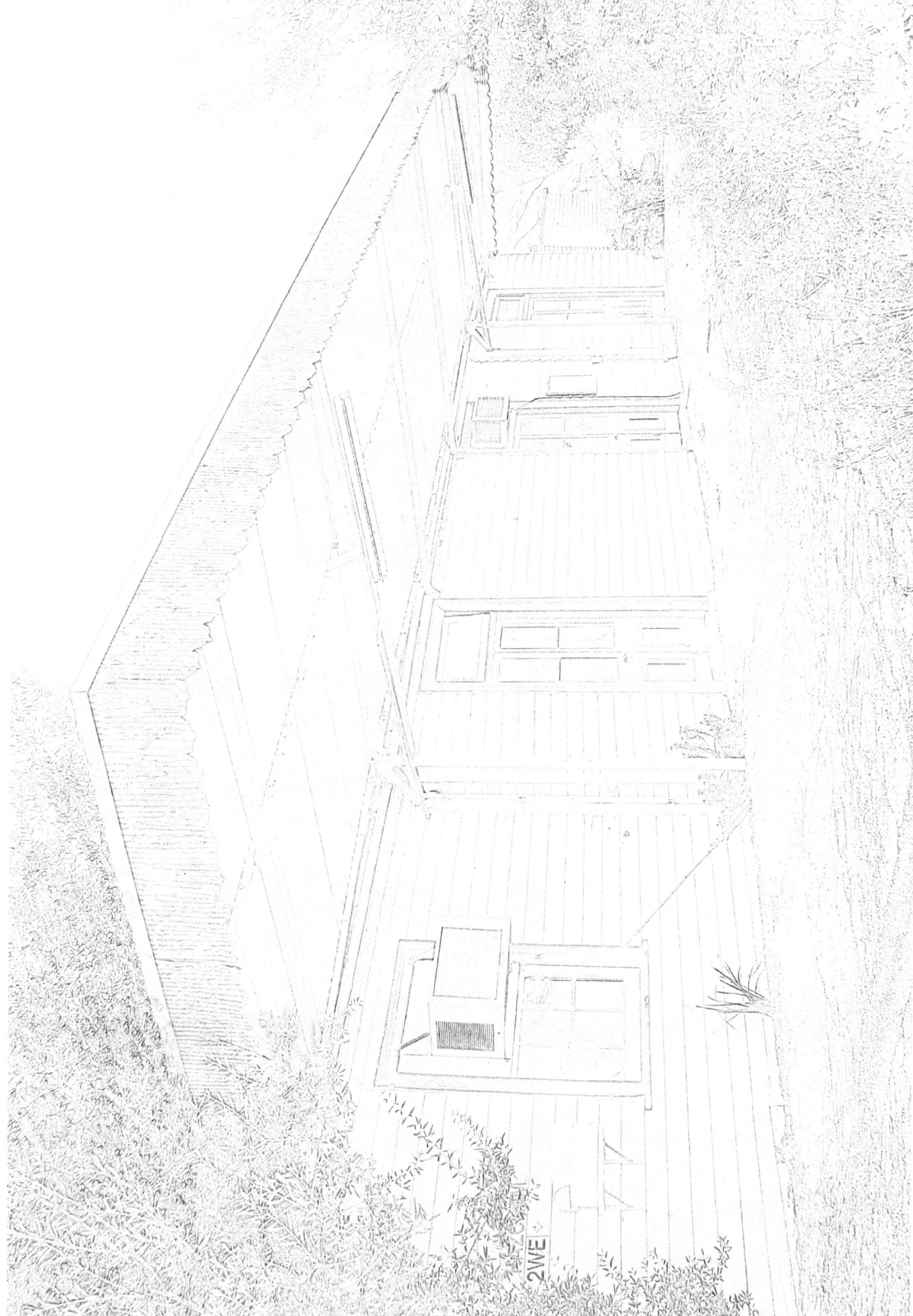

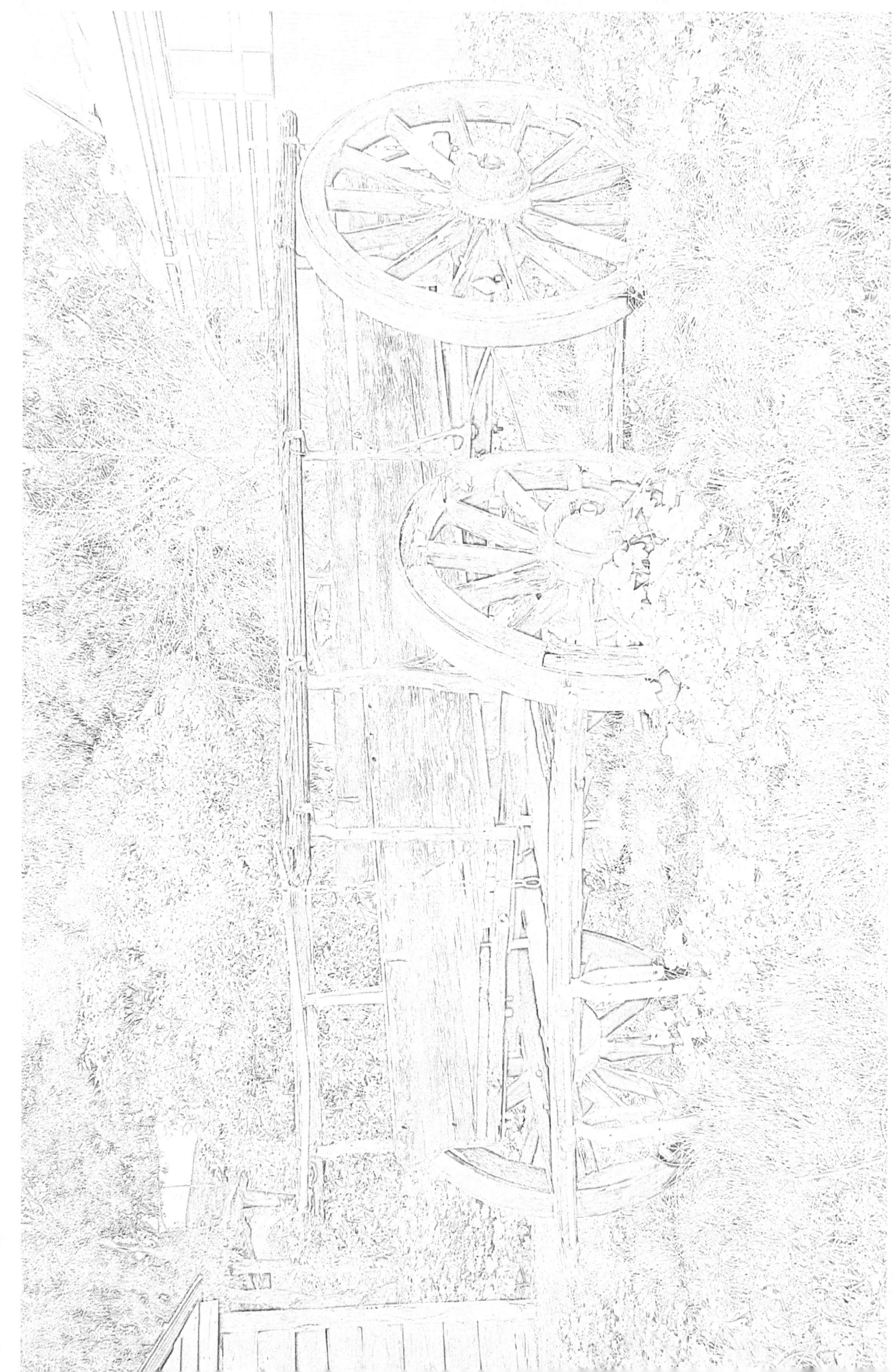

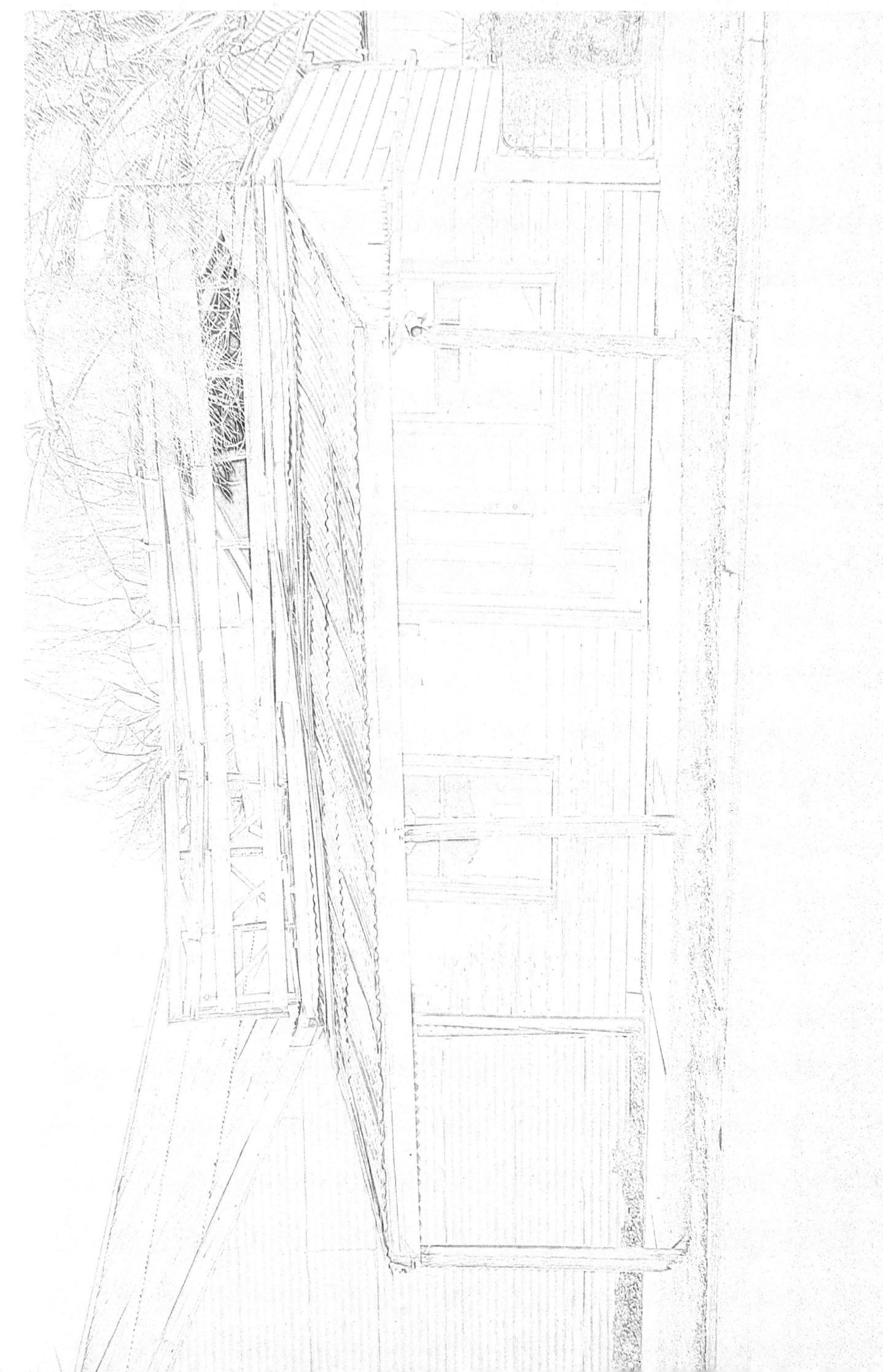

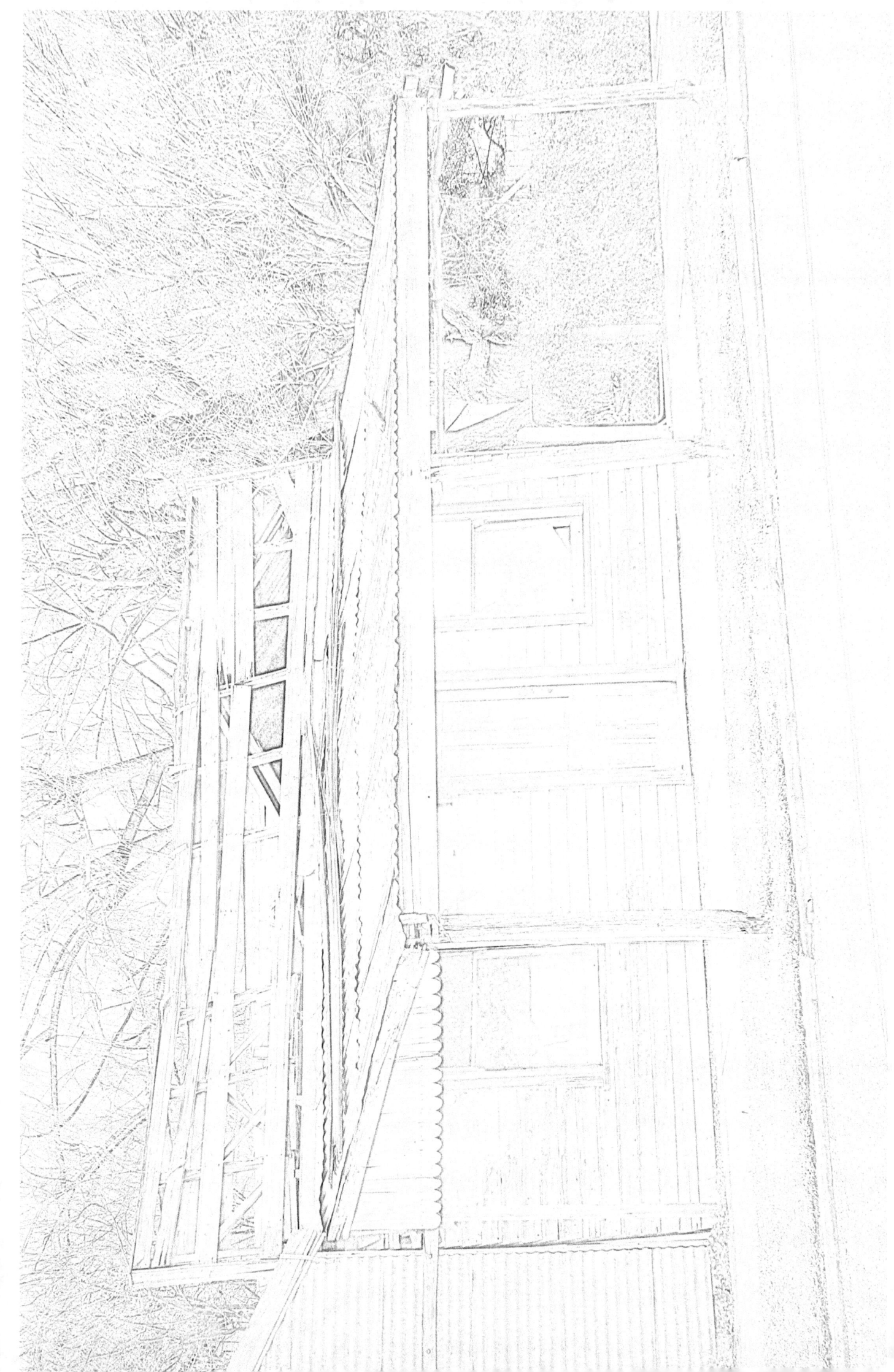

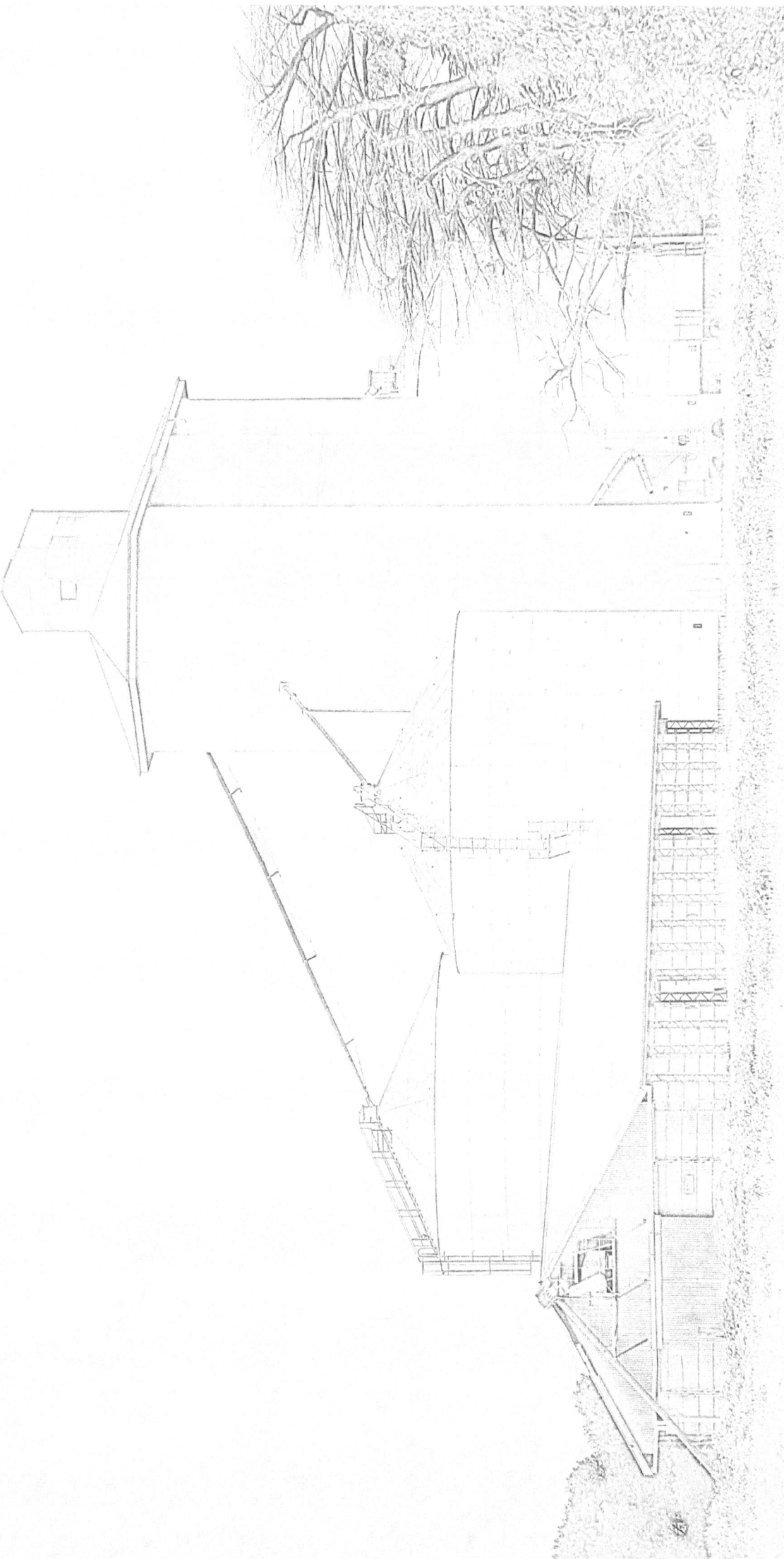

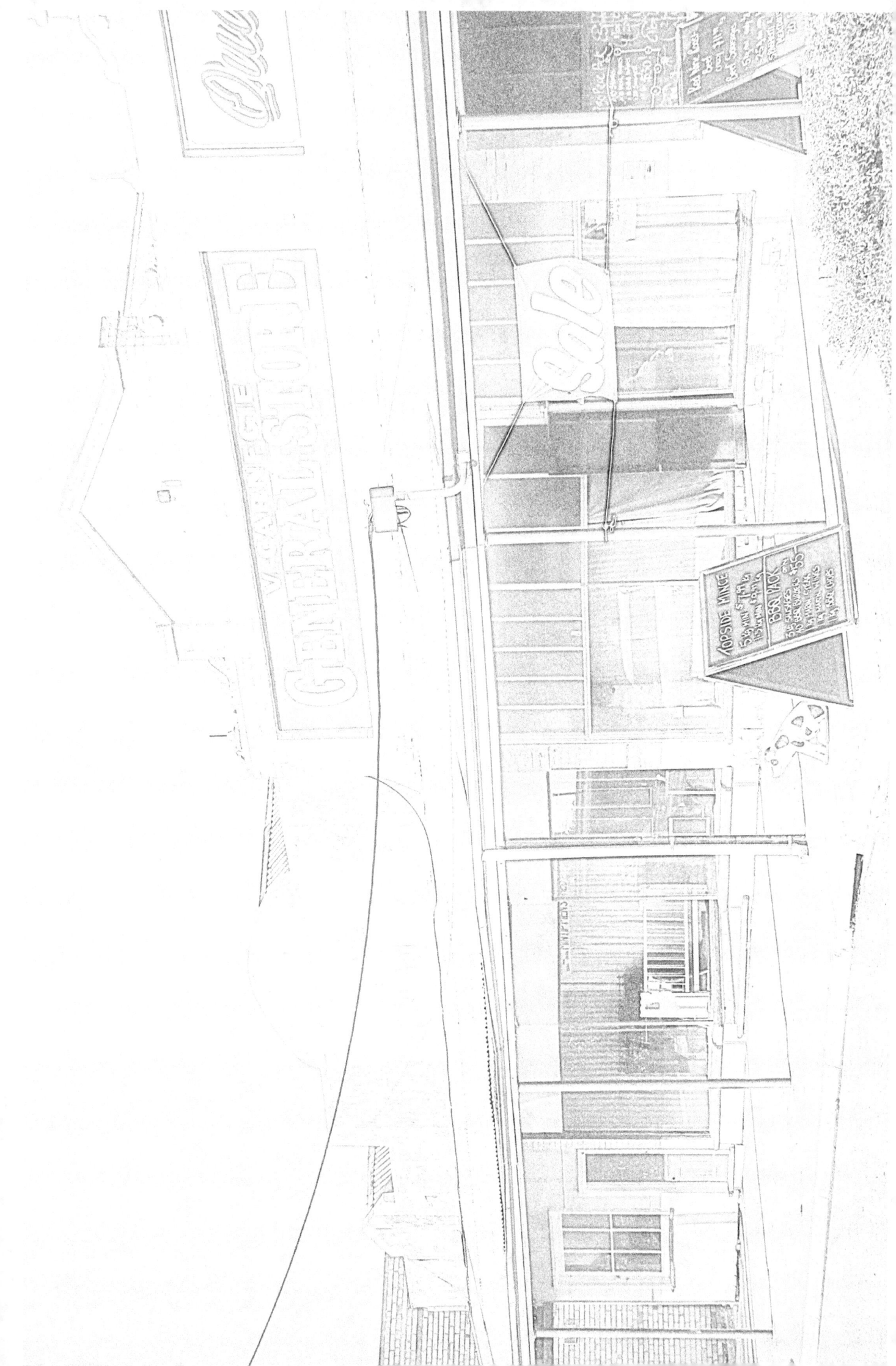

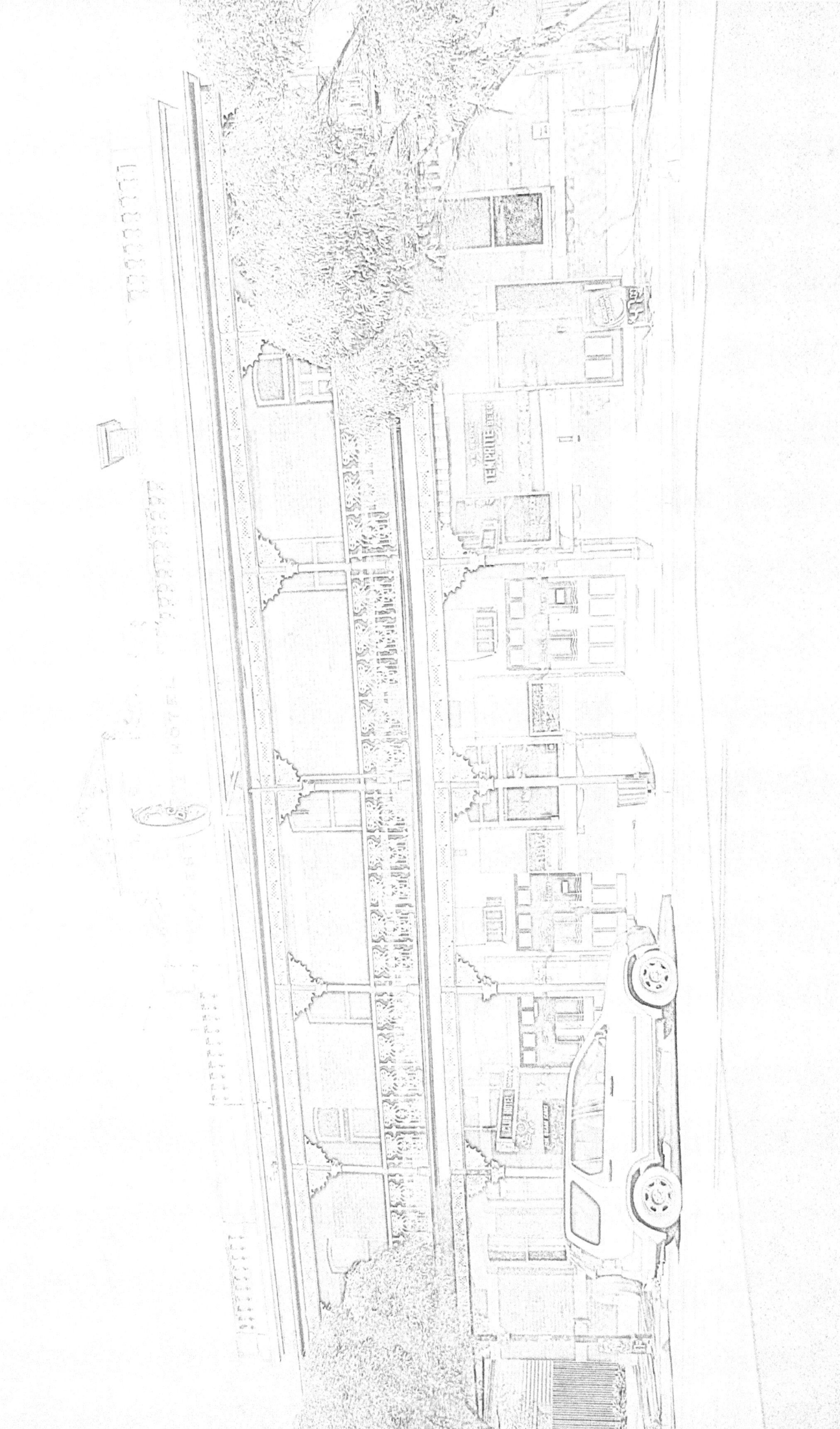

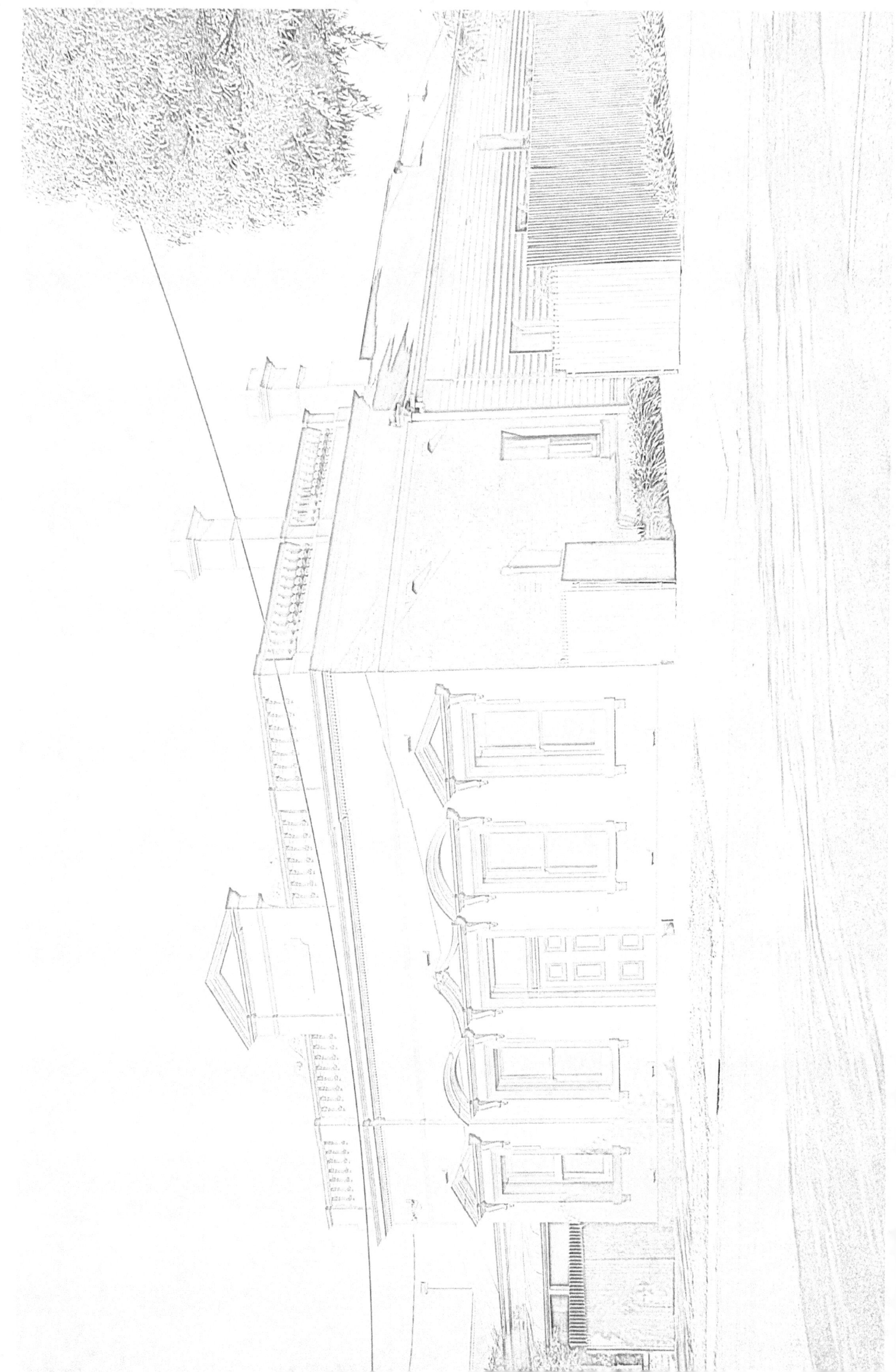

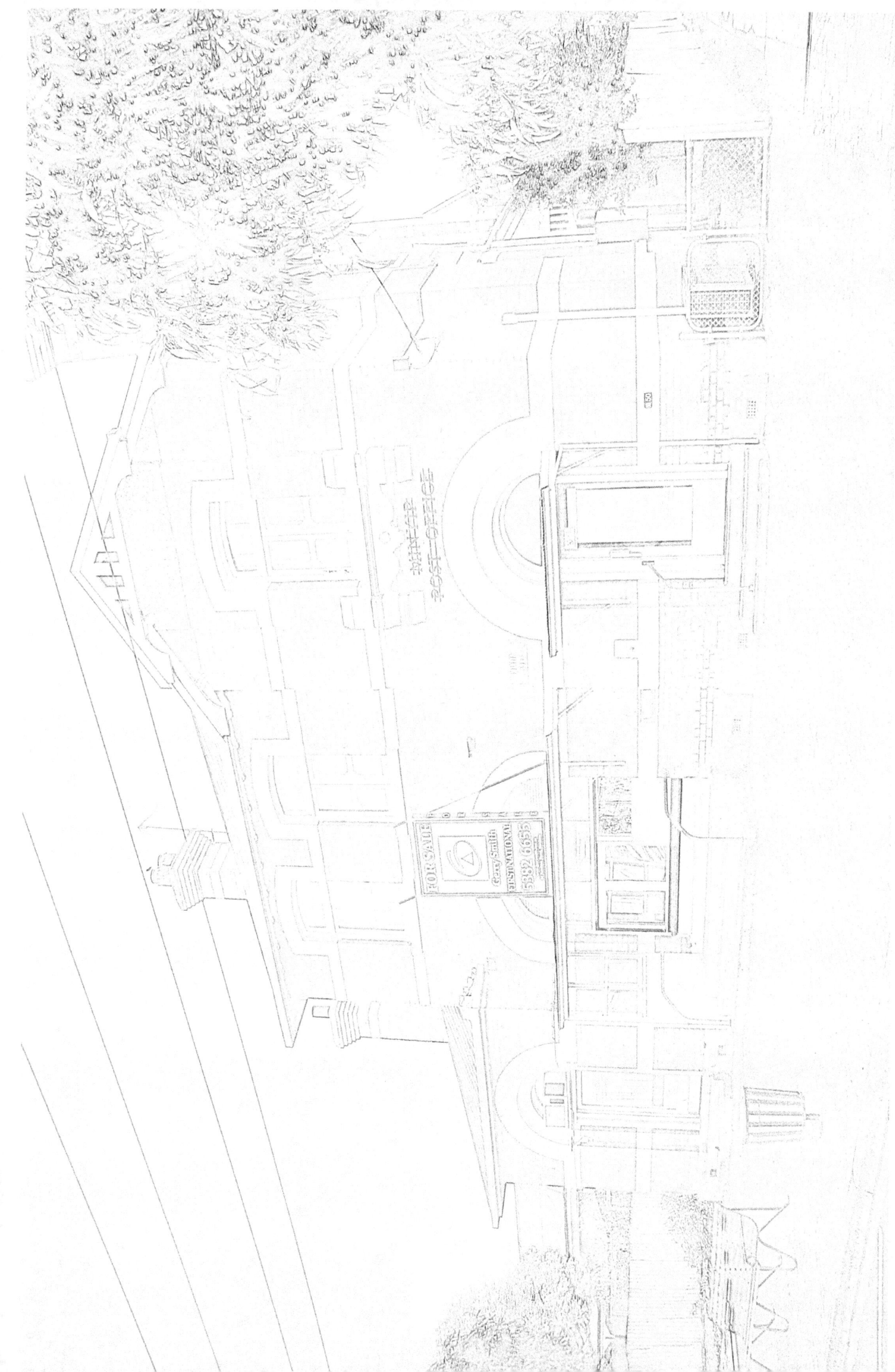

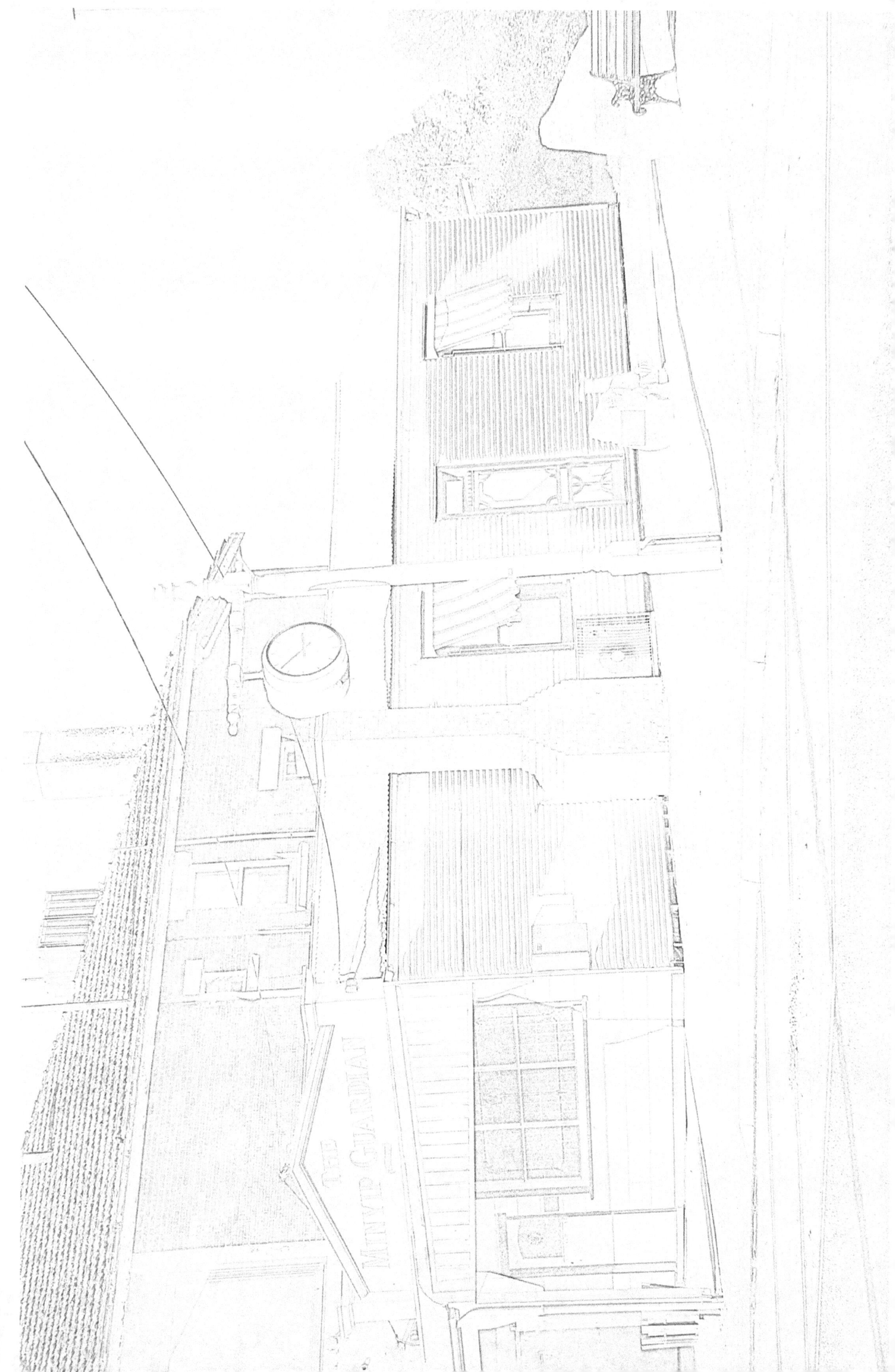

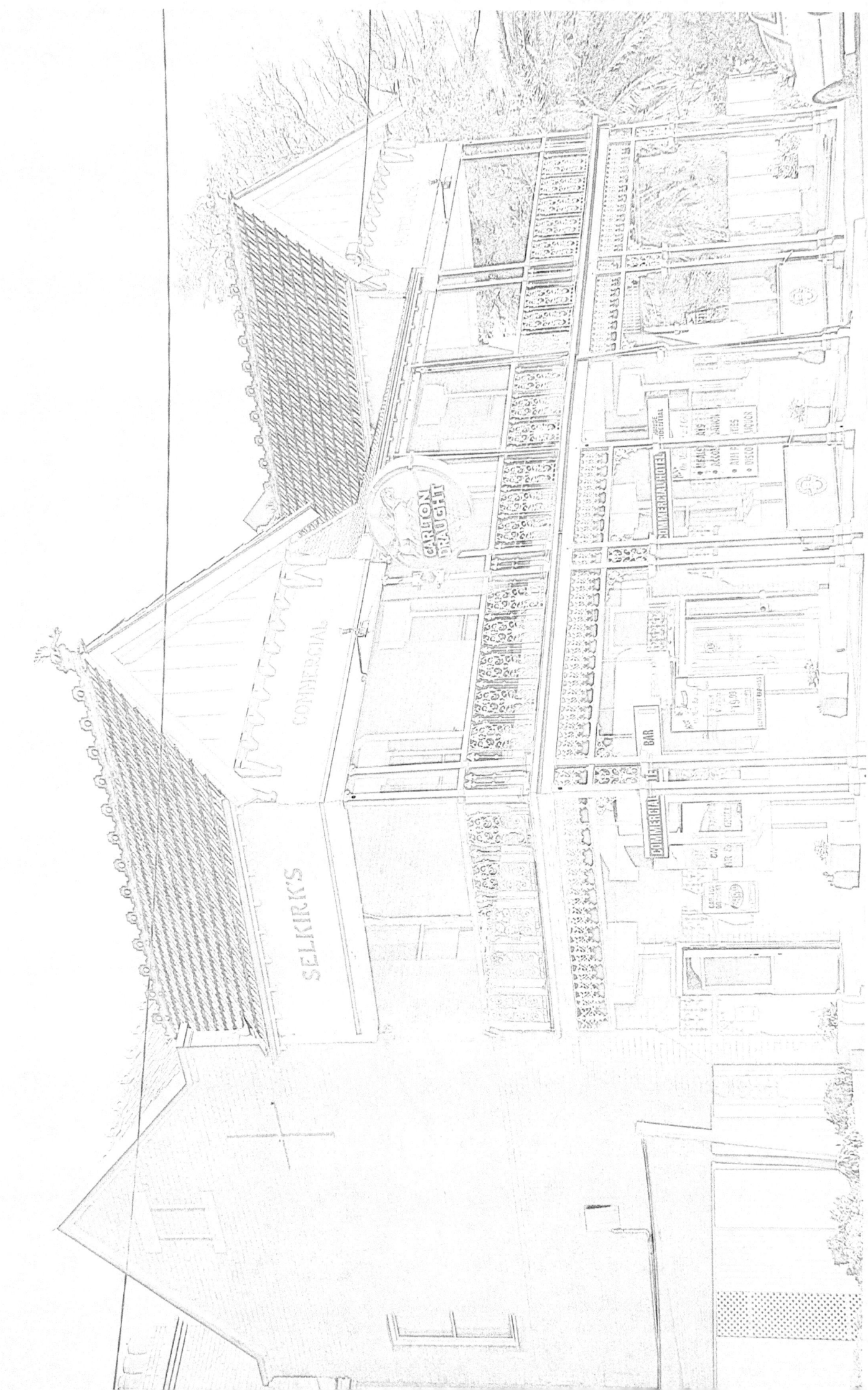

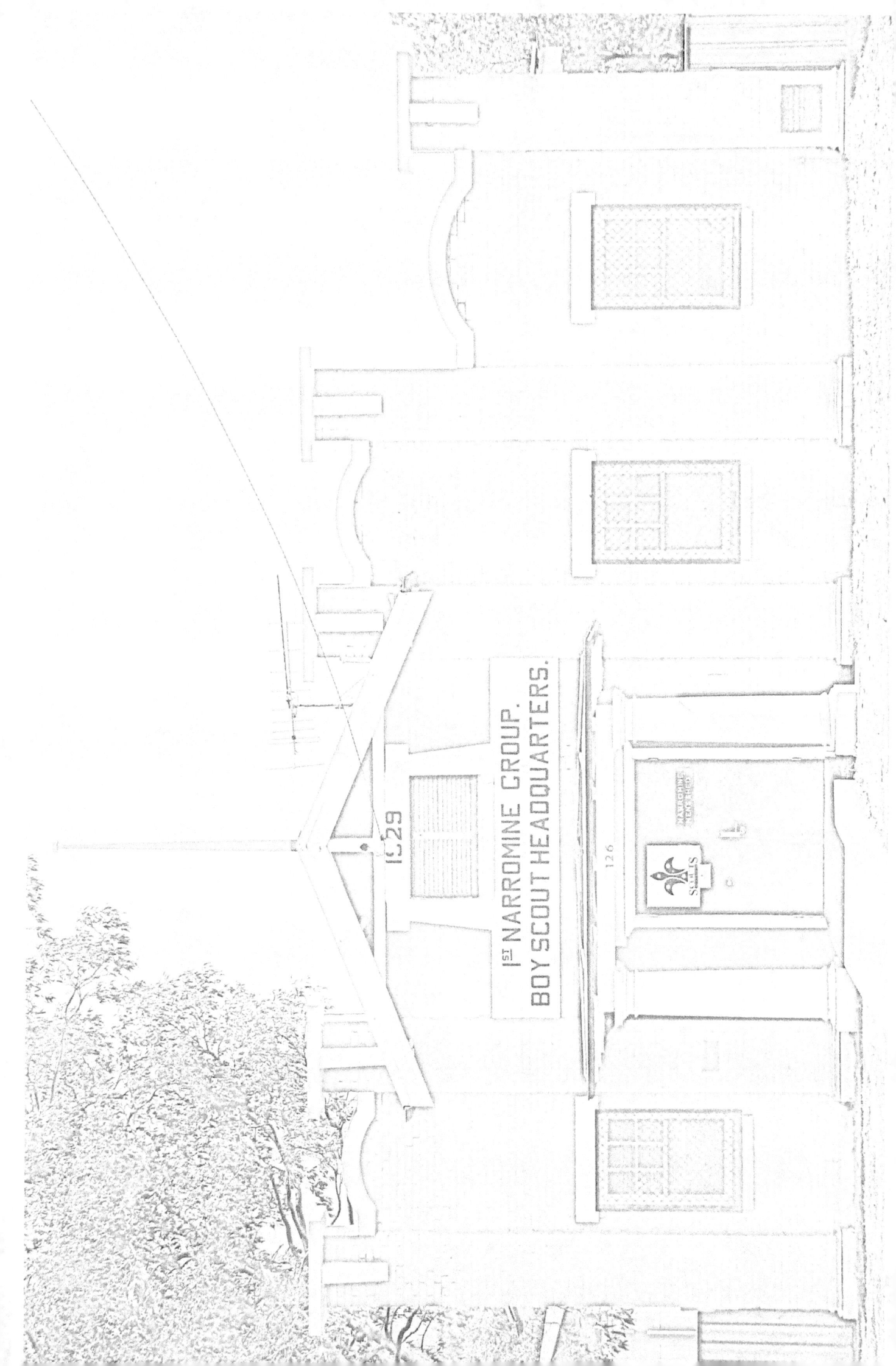

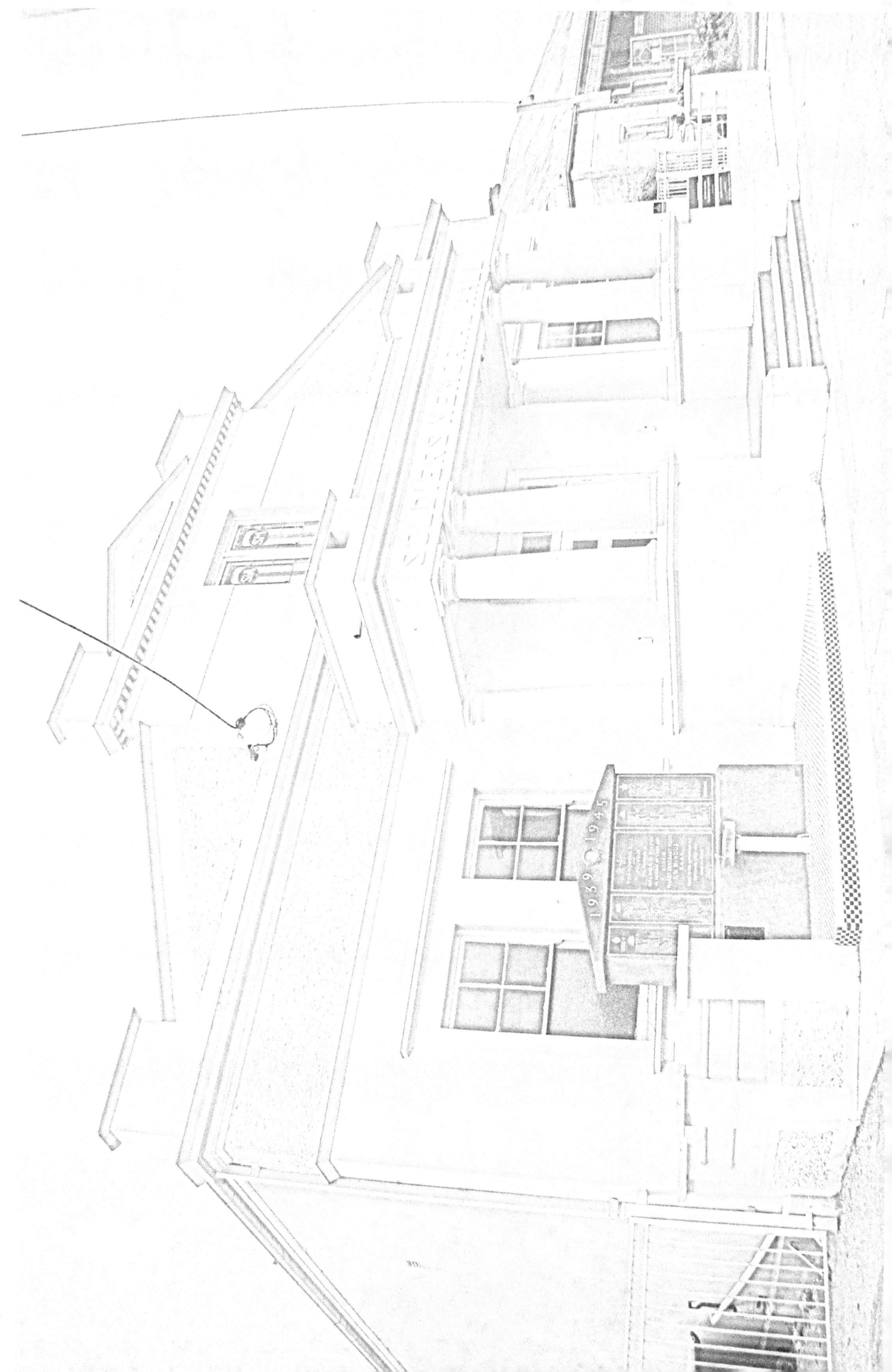

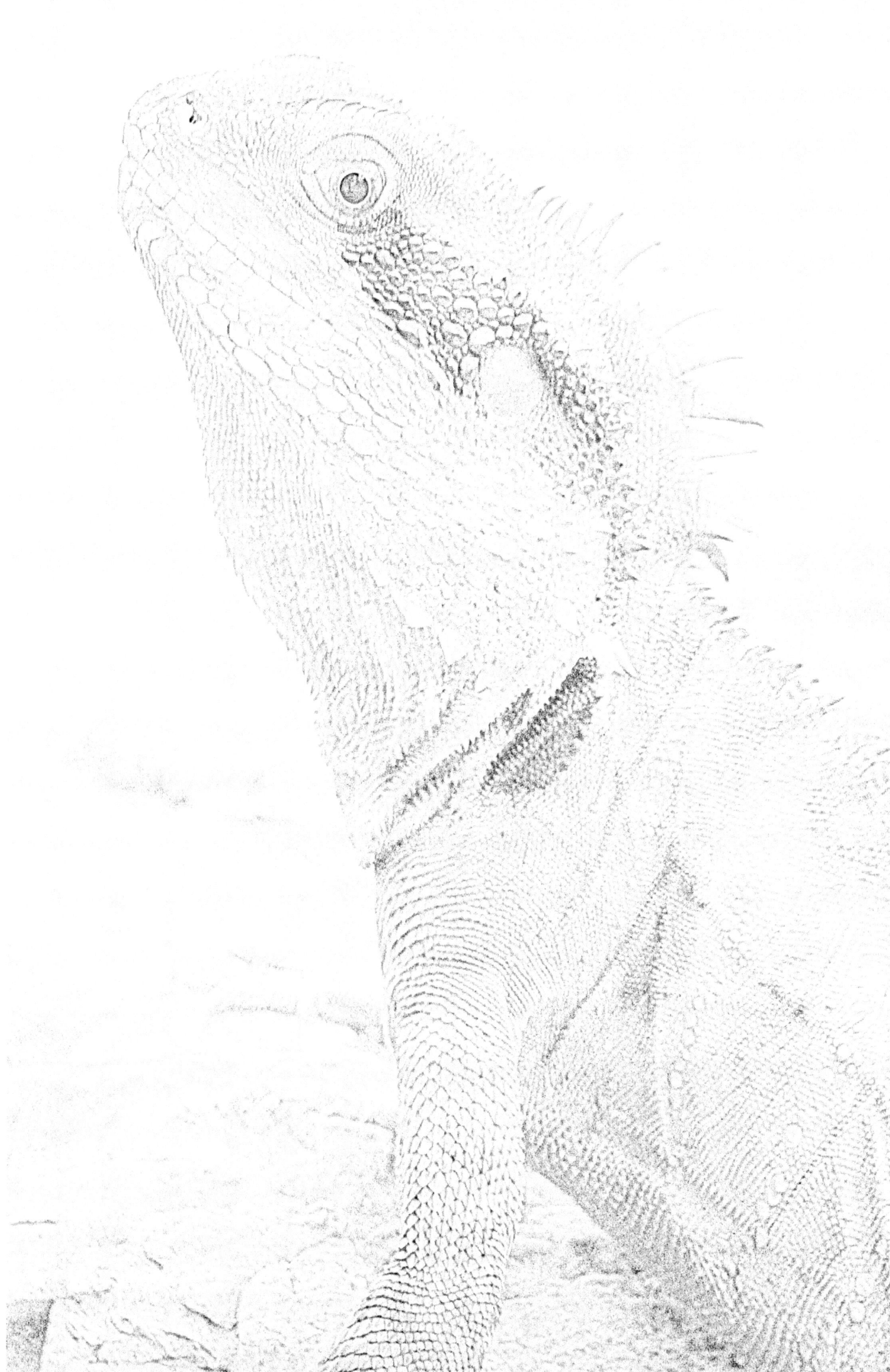

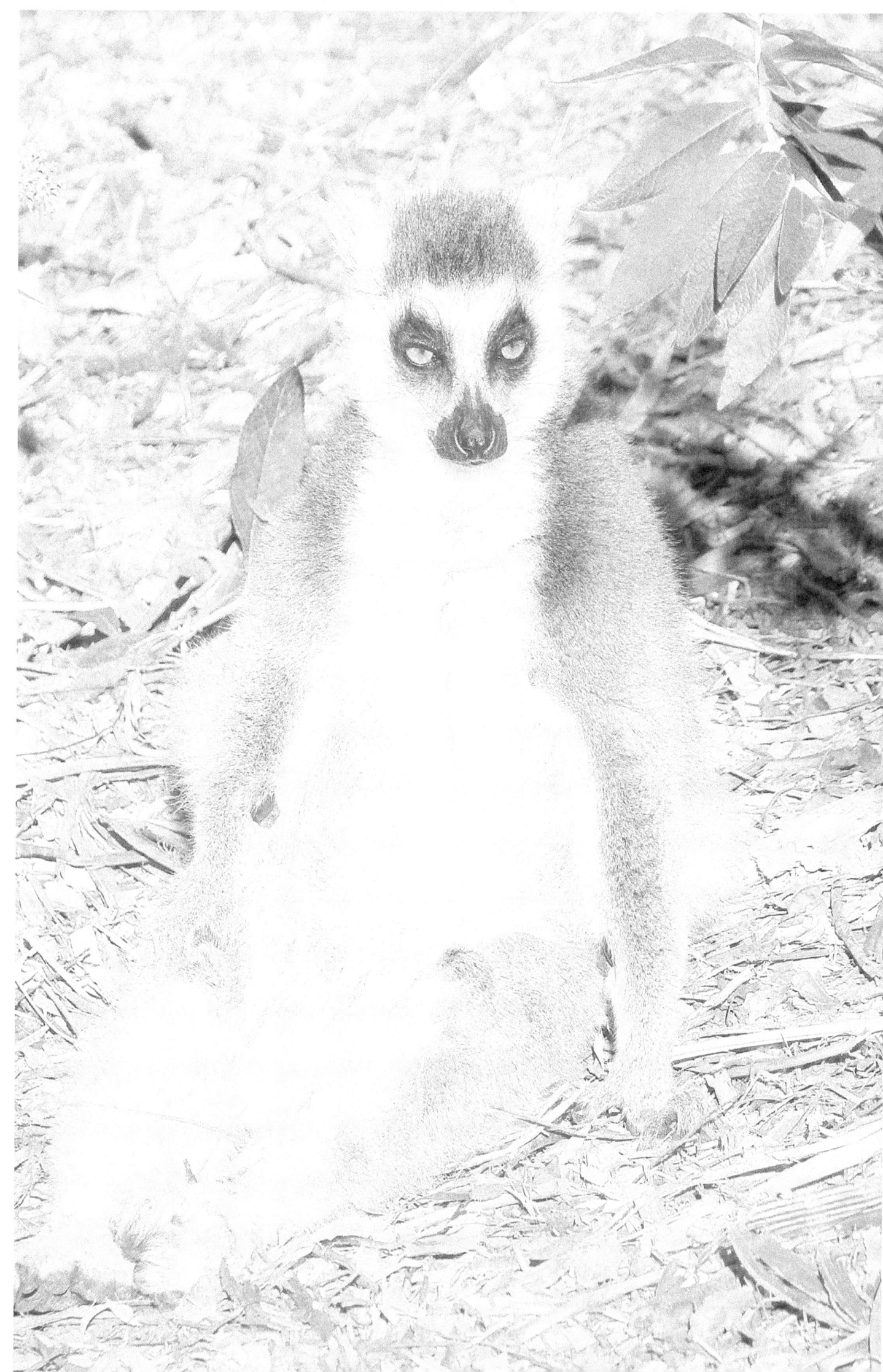

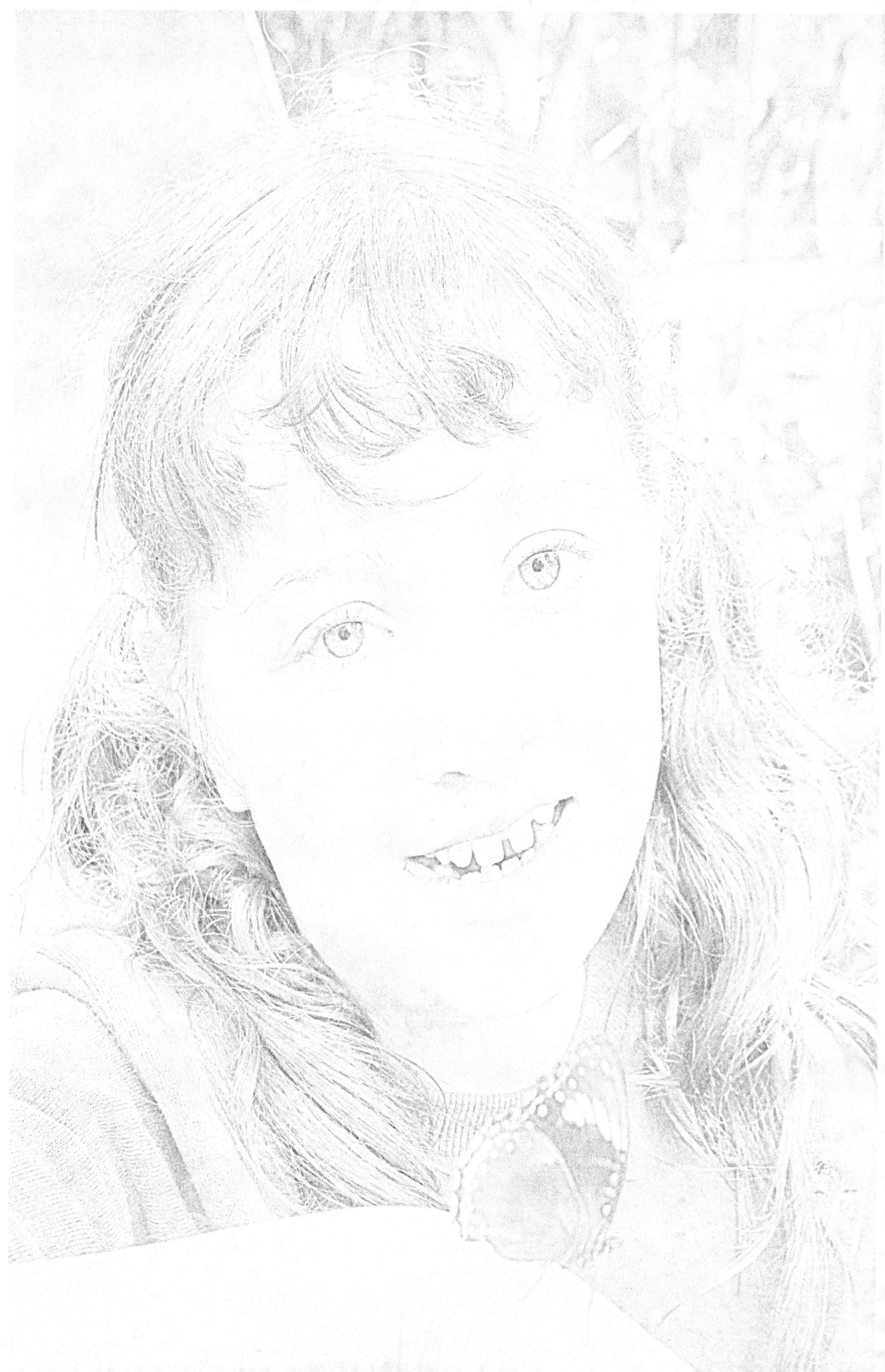